ENGLISH SHORT STORIES FOR INTERMEDIATE LEARNERS

Learn English and Build Your
Vocabulary the Fun and Easy Way

1st Edition

LANGUAGE GURU

Copyright © 2022.

All rights reserved. This book or parts thereof may not be reproduced in any form, stored in any retrieval system, or transmitted in any form by any means—electronic, mechanical, photocopy, recording, or otherwise—without prior written permission of the publisher, except as provided by United States of America copyright law.

ISBN: 978-1-950321-44-5

Medical Disclaimer:

This book is not intended as a substitute for the medical advice of doctors. The reader should regularly consult a physician in matters pertaining to their health and particularly with respect to any symptoms that may require diagnosis or medical attention.

It is recommended that you research any medical information obtained from this book with other sources. You are encouraged to confirm all information regarding any medical condition or treatment with your doctor.

The author does not assume and hereby disclaims any liabilities and responsibilities to any party for any loss, damage, or injury caused by the information in this book. This information is sold and provided with the knowledge that they do not offer any legal or other professional advice.

TABLE OF CONTENTS

Introduction..7

How to Use This Book..9

Chapter 1: 50 Days and 50 Nights..11

Chapter 2: For All the Wrong Reasons..23

Chapter 3: The Lesser of Two Evils...36

Chapter 4: The Rise of the Influencer..47

Chapter 5: Big Fish..61

Chapter 6: Magic and Might..71

Chapter 7: Mind Games...82

Chapter 8: Moderation and Extremism..97

About the Author..109

Did You Enjoy the Read?...111

Answer Key...113

INTRODUCTION

We all know that immersion is the tried and true way to learn a foreign language. After all, it's how we got so good at our first language.

The problem is that it's extremely difficult to recreate the same circumstances when we learn a foreign language. We come to rely so much on our native language for everything, and it's hard to make enough time to learn a new one.

We aren't surrounded by the foreign language in our home countries. More often than not, our families can't speak this new language we want to learn. And many of us have stressful jobs or demanding classes that eat away at our limited energy and hours of the day. Immersion can seem like an impossibility.

What we can do, however, is gradually work our way up to immersion no matter where we are in life. And the way we can do this is through extensive reading and listening.

If you have ever taken a foreign language class, chances are you are familiar with intensive reading and listening. In intensive reading and listening, a small amount of text or a short audio recording is broken down line by line, and then, you are drilled on grammar endlessly.

Extensive reading and listening, on the other hand, is quite the opposite. You read a large number of pages or listen to hours and hours of the foreign language without worrying about understanding everything. You rely on context for meaning and try to limit the number of words you need to look up.

If you ask the most successful language learners, it's not intensive but extensive reading and listening that delivers the best results. Simply, volume is much more effective than explicit explanations and rote memorization.

To be able to read like this comfortably, you must practice reading in the foreign language for hours every single day. It takes a massive volume of text before your brain stops intensively reading and shifts into extensive reading.

This book hopes to provide a few short stories in English you can use to practice extensive reading. These stories were written and edited by native English speakers from the United States. We hope these short stories help build confidence in your overall reading comprehension skills and encourage you to read more native material. They offer supplementary reading practice with a heavy focus on teaching vocabulary words.

Vocabulary is the number one barrier to entry to extensive reading. Without an active vocabulary base of 10,000 words or more, you'll be stuck constantly looking up words in the dictionary, which will be sure to slow down your reading early on. To speed up the rate at which you read, building and maintaining a vast vocabulary range is absolutely vital.

This is why it's so important to invest as much time as possible into immersing yourself in native English every single day. This includes both reading and listening as well as being around native speakers through any and all means possible.

We hope you enjoy the book and find it useful in growing your English vocabulary and bringing you a few steps closer to extensive reading and fluency!

HOW TO USE THIS BOOK

To simulate extensive reading better, we recommend keeping things simple and using the short stories in the following manner. Read through each story just once and no more. Whenever you encounter a word you don't know, first try to guess its meaning using the surrounding context. If its meaning is still unclear and the word is in **bold**, check that chapter's vocabulary and grammar list for a very simplified definition. If the unknown word is not in bold, a quick online dictionary search may be required.

In our vocabulary lists, we have strived both to include as many potentially new words and phrases as possible but also to keep each list as brief as possible. As a result, we left out a great deal of words that can be understood via context as well as many basic words.

In addition, it's also recommended to read each story silently. While reading aloud can seem beneficial for pronunciation and intonation, it's a practice more aligned with intensive reading. It will further slow down your reading pace and make it considerably more difficult for you to get into extensive reading.

If you want to work on pronunciation and intonation, consider practicing these during study and review times rather than reading time. Alternatively, you could also speak to a English tutor or friend to practice what you learned.

After completing the reading for each chapter, test your knowledge of the story by answering the comprehension questions. Check your answers using the answer key located at the end of the book.

As a means of review, memorization of any kind is completely unnecessary for language acquisition. The actual language acquisition process occurs subconsciously, and any effort to memorize new vocabulary and grammar structures only stores this information in your short-term memory. Attempting to force new information into your long-term memory only serves to eat up your time and make it that much more frustrating when you can't recall it in the future.

If you wish to review new information that you have learned from the short stories, there are several options that would be wiser. Spaced Repetition Systems (SRS) allow you to cut down on your review time by setting specific intervals in which you are tested on information in order to promote long-term memory storage. Anki and the Goldlist Method are two popular SRS choices that give you the ability to review whatever information you'd like from whatever material you'd like.

Trying to actively review every single new thing you learn, however, will slow you down on your overall path to fluency. While there may be hundreds or even thousands of sentences you want to practice and review, perhaps the best way to go about internalizing it all is to forget it. If it's that important, it will come up through more reading and listening to more English. Languages are more effectively acquired when we allow ourselves to read and listen to them naturally.

And with that, it is time to get started with the eight stories presented in this volume. Good luck to you, reader!

CHAPTER ONE:

50 DAYS AND 50 NIGHTS

David was a **mess. Going through** a **divorce** meant the end of a life he spent 20 years building. His emotions were **drained** of all life, and there was no energy or **desire** to do anything.

Instead, there was only pain. A **force** that could not be seen **ate away at** him at every hour of every day. A feeling of **hopelessness** was **consuming** him slowly, and one day there would be nothing left of him.

Fear was the only thing that moved David out of bed and to work each morning. It was a fear of things becoming worse than they already were. And they could always get worse. He could get fired, become poor, lose his home, or even get **addicted** to drugs. Any of those could be **the last straw**.

There were only two **comforts** left in the world: food and sleep. While sleep completely **numbed** the pain, food only provided a short **distraction**. Corn chips, lasagna, cookies, pizza, and **greasy** burgers and fries were the **go-tos**. The sugars, fats, and salts **flooded** the pleasure centers of his brain while his **soul** felt no such thing.

David would eat and eat until he could eat no more. And then, he would return right back to the **despair** he was in before. And each time, the despair would be **coupled with disgust** of himself. There was nothing he could do but suffer. When sleep finally did come, it was a **mercy**.

Since the start of the **separation** with his **ex-wife**, David's weight had **jumped** from 190 to 260 pounds. He knew he was in bad health. He could feel it. He would die of **heart failure** or of something soon. This he knew.

And then, one day, David **came across** a story and a community he would never imagine to be real. Through social media, he learned that a group of **dedicated** individuals online were doing **fasts** lasting from 24 hours to 30 days or more.

The story was told in a post by a man who completely **transformed** his life by completing a 40-day fast. At first, David was **alarmed**. But he soon saw that it was all done **under** medical **supervision**. It was like something **straight out** of **the Bible** but achieved by a normal human. And in his post, there were tips for anyone who wanted to **accomplish** the same.

David **was more than sold**. He would try a water fast and go for as long as he could. He would drink only liquids that contained no calories and eat no food. The thought **alone** of eating disgusted him, so he had plenty of **motivation** to get started.

The first morning without breakfast felt strange, but there was no **turning back** now. Besides, David could still have his morning coffee, and that first cup was often the highlight of his day.

This time, though, he had to drink it black, which he was not used to. After his first **sip**, he immediately missed the milky and sugary flavors he was so used to. But at the same time, this **sacrifice** had meaning. Learning to **go without** meant everything to him.

Lunch and dinner were equally strange. David was so used to eating during these times that it was hard to do something different. But he realized something. He wasn't actually hungry. He had more than plenty of food the day before, so he just needed to find something to focus on and **bide his time**.

New **coping mechanisms** were required. Walking and drinking water became David's new best friends. Anytime he felt the **urge** to eat, he would **walk it off**. He also sipped on water **constantly**.

The best part was that he didn't have to workout to lose weight. The fasting and walking did the **heavy lifting** for him.

Having an **appetite** but being unable to eat was annoying, but eventually it would go away. It never lasted. **Cravings** came and went. If he could just be with those feelings for long enough without **giving in** to them, they would pass.

Day three was a challenge. There was a stress that slowly **built up** throughout the day after not eating for so long. By dinner time, it became **unbearable**. David had previously **stowed away** a bag of chips deep in his **pantry** behind healthier choices. It was an effort to forget they ever existed. But in this moment, he remembered exactly where they were and went to **retrieve** them. He was near determined to break the fast.

Out of desperation, he focused on the stress he was currently feeling. He asked himself if this was worse than the past year of **hell** he had gone through. He had already suffered so much, to many points he did not think he could live through. This one moment of stress was nothing compared to any of that. If he could somehow go through that and live, he could somehow be with this level of stress.

And so he **set** his **temptation aside** and lay down on his couch. He **tossed**. He **turned**. He suffered. But he did so with purpose. He was unsure if the hunger **pangs** would go away. Yet by the time night had come, the hunger had passed, and he was **shocked**.

After that day, all of his hunger **ceased** to exist, and the fast became **significantly** easier. A week passed. And then another week passed.

Of course, David kept well **hydrated**. He drank plenty of **electrolyte** drinks to **maintain** good energy levels. He also saw his doctor each week to **monitor** his health and make sure everything was OK.

A month into the fast, David was **astounded**. How could someone still have energy despite having no food **whatsoever**? His body still had so much energy to burn due to his size. If he could go this long without food, it made him **rethink** the reason why he ate. It must have been **boredom** and the desire to not sit there and be with that boredom, he figured.

Soon enough, day 50 had come. There was no specific number of days he aimed for, however. David's original goal was simply to fast for as long as he possibly could. With all the improvements in his health and energy he had seen these past 50 days, he certainly could continue. He thought he could even run a mile or two with how good he felt.

Realizing he had achieved what he really wanted out of all of this, David decided to finally break his fast but very slowly and carefully. His doctor had warned him that eating too many calories too quickly after a **prolonged** fast could cause him to die. This is because of the **rapid** change in electrolyte levels that would occur. It causes very serious health **complications**. This process is called **Refeeding Syndrome**.

At the doctor's office, his electrolyte levels were checked with a blood test. He was advised to only **consume** a small amount of calories each day for the next week. Easily **digestible** fruits like **watermelon** and apples were to be his first few meals. **Citrus** fruits were to be avoided **at all costs**. He was also recommended to take a **vitamin supplement**. If all went well after the first few meals, he could start eating vegetables like **sauerkraut**.

So on the morning of day 51, David sliced up a watermelon and grabbed a fork, ready to eat. He carefully **handpicked** his first piece of food after 50 days. He then brought the **chunk** of melon close to his lips. Opening his mouth, he **leaned** in to take a bite. But he stopped himself and smiled out of **nervousness**. Trying again only got him the same result. It was as if he had forgotten how to eat.

He **countdown** from three. On zero, he **plunged** the fruit **into** his mouth and started **chewing**. It was like recovering a lost memory from years past. Once again, he remembered what it was like to taste something incredibly sweet. And it was **pure joy**.

One thing was clear now. Food was a gift. Food was something to be enjoyed. It was not a prison, and he was not its prisoner.

It was all as if David had been given a second chance at life. And so he was ready to continue living. This time he **carried** not only a lot less weight but all the experience and **wisdom** of the past.

Vocabulary and Grammar

- **mess** *(informal)* --- a person that is full of problems

- **go through** *(experience)* --- to experience something difficult

- **divorce** --- the formal end of a marriage

- **drained** --- extremely tired with no energy

- **desire** *[noun]* --- a strong feeling of wanting something

- **force** *(influence)* --- (a person/thing that has) power or influence
- **eat away at sth.** --- to reduce or destroy sth. slowly over time
- **hopelessness** *(feeling)* --- the feeling of being without hope
- **consume** *(destroy)* --- to completely destroy something
- **addicted** --- unable to stop using or doing something
- **the last straw** --- the last thing in a series that makes you change
- **comfort** *(help)* --- sth. that makes you feel less sad, worried, or pain
- **numb** *[verb]* --- to make somebody unable to feel something
- **distraction** --- sth. that takes away your attention from sth. else
- **greasy** --- covered in fat or oil
- **go-to** --- a person or thing that somebody often goes to or uses
- **flood** *[verb]* --- to fill a place in large numbers
- **soul** --- the part of a person that some believe exists after death
- **despair** *[noun]* --- the feeling of losing or having no hope
- **coupled with** --- combined with something
- **disgust** *[noun]* --- a strong feeling of really not liking something
- **mercy** *(event)* --- an event that stops or prevents suffering
- **separation** *(law)* --- a decision to stay married but live separately
- **ex-wife** --- a woman someone was once married to
- **jump** *(increase)* --- to suddenly increase by a lot
- **heart failure** --- a condition where the heart does not work well

- **come across** *(find)* --- to find someone or something by chance
- **dedicated** *(committed)* --- putting a lot of time and energy into sth.
- **fast** *[noun]* --- a long period of time where you don't eat
- **transform** --- to completely change the form or appearance of sth.
- **alarmed** --- frightened or worried by something
- **under** *(experiencing)* --- happening during a particular process
- **supervision** --- watching sb. to make sure everything is OK
- **straight out** --- simply and directly
- **the Bible** --- the book of the Christian religion
- **accomplish** --- to achieve or finish doing something
- **be sold on something** --- to be convinced about something
- **more than** --- very
- **alone** *(emphasis)* --- used to say the whole problem is much greater
- **motivation** *(feeling)* --- a strong feeling of wanting to do sth.
- **turn back** --- to return the way you came or make sb. do this
- **sip** *[noun]* --- a small amount of a drink you take into your mouth
- **sacrifice** *(giving up)* --- giving up sth. important for sth. more important
- **go without** --- to manage without something you usually have
- **bide your time** --- to wait for a good time to do something
- **cope** --- to deal with a difficult situation successfully
- **mechanism** *(method)* --- a method or system for achieving sth.

- **urge** *[noun]* --- a strong desire for sth. that is hard to control
- **walk something off** --- to walk in order to get rid of a feeling
- **constantly** --- all the time
- **heavy lifting** *[idiom]* --- hard work
- **appetite** *(food)* --- the feeling of wanting to eat
- **craving** --- the feeling of really wanting something
- **give in** --- to admit defeat or to finally agree to what sb. wants
- **build up** --- to become larger or stronger or make sth. do this
- **unbearable** --- too painful or unpleasant to be with
- **stow away sth.** --- to put sth. in a safe place for a future time
- **pantry** --- a large cupboard or small room used to store food
- **retrieve** --- to find and bring something back
- **out of** *(because of)* --- used to show why somebody does sth.
- **desperation** --- when you are willing to do *anything* in a bad situation
- **hell** *(situation)* --- an extremely bad experience full of suffering
- **set aside** *(ignore)* --- to ignore sth. because sth. else is more important
- **temptation** *(desire)* --- the desire to do or have sth. that is bad
- **toss and turn** --- to move around in bed because you can't sleep
- **pang** --- a sudden strong feeling of pain
- **shock** *(surprise)* *[verb]* --- to make sb. feel surprised or upset
- **cease** --- *(formal)* to stop

- **significantly** *(greatly)* --- in a way that is large or important
- **hydrated** --- having enough water
- **electrolyte** *(nutrition)* --- an important mineral for your body
- **maintain** *(keep up)* --- to make sth. continue at the same level
- **monitor** *[verb]* --- to watch and check something over time
- **astounded** --- very shocked or surprised
- **whatsoever** --- (none) at all
- **rethink** --- to think about sth. again in order to change sth.
- **boredom** --- the times when we are bored
- **prolonged** --- continuing for a long time
- **rapid** --- fast
- **complication** --- something that makes a situation more difficult
- **refeed** --- to feed again after a long period of little to no food
- **syndrome** *(medical)* --- used to name some illnesses
- **consume** *(eat)* --- to eat or drink
- **digestible** *(food)* --- easy to change from food to sth. your body can use
- **watermelon** --- a big green fruit with a red inside and black seeds
- **citrus** --- fruits like oranges, lemons, limes, and grapefruits
- **at all costs** --- used to say something must be done
- **vitamin** --- a substance found in food that is needed to be healthy
- **supplement** --- sth. that is added to sth. else to complete or improve it

- **sauerkraut** --- cabbage that has been cut, salted, and sitting in a jar
- **handpick** --- to carefully choose for a special purpose
- **chunk** --- a large piece that has been cut or broken off
- **lean** --- to move one side of something towards one direction
- **nervousness** --- the feeling of being nervous
- **countdown [verb]** --- to count down time until sth. important happens
- **plunge sth. into sth.** --- to push sth. into sth. else suddenly
- **chew** --- to bite into something again and again
- **pure** *(total)* --- total and complete
- **joy** *(happiness)* --- a very strong feeling of being happy
- **carry** *(quality)* --- to have something as a quality or a result
- **wisdom** --- the ability to use experience to make smart decisions

50 Days and 50 Nights

Comprehension Questions

1. Why was David's life falling apart?
    A) He was going through a breakup with his ex-girlfriend.
    B) He was going through a divorce.
    C) He was going to attend a funeral.
    D) He was going through bankruptcy.

2. How did food and sleep help David cope with his feelings?
    A) Sleep numbed the pain, and food was an abstraction.
    B) Sleep softened the pain, and food was a distraction.
    C) Food was an abstraction, and sleep softened the pain.
    D) Food was a distraction, and sleep numbed the pain.

3. If something was done under medical supervision, it means...
    A) it was done while a doctor monitored the situation.
    B) it was done while a doctor recommended supplements.
    C) it was done while a doctor checked your electrolyte levels.
    D) it was done while a doctor advised you on the complications.

4. Where did David's motivation to start fasting come from?
    A) He was disgusted with his thoughts while eating alone
    B) He was disgusted just by the thought of eating
    C) He was disgusted by thoughts that were eating at him
    D) He was disgusted by the thought of being alone and eating

5. What sacrifice did David make in the morning?
    A) Learning to go without breakfast
    B) Having milk and sugar at his house
    C) Drinking coffee with cream and sugar
    D) His livestock in the name of the Aztec gods

6. Which were NOT new coping mechanisms David learned?
   A) Finding something to focus on and biding his time
   B) Being with his appetite and cravings until they passed
   C) Doing heavy lifting while fasting and walking
   D) Sipping water and going for walks

7. What happened on the third day?
   A) David battled the temptation to eat due to rising stress.
   B) David suffered and endured through hell.
   C) David battled his issues with his ex-wife while on the couch.
   D) David's stress had built up, so he snacked on a bag of chips.

8. How did David have so much energy despite eating no food?
   A) He had a doctor monitor his health.
   B) He drank lots of electrolytes and also because of his size.
   C) He was well hydrated and astounded.
   D) He figured out that he ate mostly because he was bored.

9. Why did David decide to break the fast?
   A) He fasted for as long as he could.
   B) He accomplished what he really wanted from fasting.
   C) He thought he could run a mile or two.
   D) Eating too many calories after a long fast could kill him.

10. Why should you eat small meals first after a prolonged fast?
    A) Your doctor has to check your electrolyte levels first.
    B) Your doctor has to give you digestible medication.
    C) You have to take a vitamin supplement first.
    D) You can die from complications from Refeeding Syndrome.

CHAPTER TWO:

FOR ALL THE WRONG REASONS

Ever since she was a teenager, Amy knew she was **destined** to be a writer. Even as a child, there was this **magnetic** attraction that **drew** her into the world of books.

She **devoured** story after story. Her parents had no trouble buying her more for her reading habit. It was an easy **investment** that was **relatively** cheap. And it would most definitely **pay off** in the near future. Amy's growing desire to write, however, would **go unrecognized**.

Her parents saw her **obsession** with reading fiction as a sign of high **intellect**. So they made a team effort to push her into focusing her time and effort into school. Soon, there wasn't as much time for Amy to read her newest novels because she had piano and math classes to attend after school. Amy had no **objection** to these extra classes. She was told by her mother and father that she was incredibly **gifted** with talents that not many other kids had. And it would be **a shame** to let all her natural abilities waste away when they could be used for good.

When Amy entered high school, the pressure began to **escalate** further. She was expected to make **straight A's** every semester. To make sure she was performing at her best, her mother would quiz her every day on what she learned. Amy would also have to explain what she was learning in all her classes. When she couldn't **recall** important details, her mother would always smile and **crack a joke**.

She was never **straight-up** mean with her daughter. Her intentions were **cleverly disguised** with love and a silly character. Amy knew, however, that it was her mother's **indirect** way of letting her know what she needed to study that night. She would be quizzed later that night to make sure she absolutely knew the information by the next day.

All the extra **schooling** and study sessions did not leave Amy with much time for a social life. When she did have an hour or two to herself, she would rather **pick up** where she left off in the last book she was reading. Her father **rewarded** her with a few new novels with every report card she brought to him. And it would always be straight A's. She never disappointed her parents' **expectations**.

Those few spare moments when she was reading seemed to pass by far too quickly. Pages would **fly** as she **raced against the clock** to make as much progress as she could. There never seemed to be enough time, however. For the hours she was reading, time did not exist. Amy would be **immersed** in worlds authors created.

Its characters had new levels of **complexity** with every chapter she read. **There was something about** how people presented themselves. Sometimes their actions did not **align** with their public image. Authors could also **reveal** actions that were hidden from other characters. If done well enough, she would start to care about what happens to certain people in the story. This process completely **fascinated** Amy.

College would **prove** to **push** her away from her obsession. The **freedom** that came with living away from home was certainly welcomed, though. How she spent her time was her decision and hers alone.

On campus and in the **dorm** rooms, Amy finally had the chance to **socialize** with other students. From **party animals** to young **geniuses**, there were all kinds of people she had the opportunity to meet. This included **entrepreneurs** who had big ideas to make big companies. Also included were athletes who had strength and abilities she did not even know were possible. And of course, a large percentage of students she met **were in the same boat** as her. They were **floating around** trying to **find their place** in society.

Amy dreamed of becoming a famous writer, but it was a dream with many risks attached. Not many writers **made it big**, after all. Many who **pursued** the dream couldn't **land a deal** with a major publisher. She heard hundreds of stories from writers who spent years writing novels only to be **turned down** by everybody. These writers ended up working **dead-end jobs** just to pay the bills. In this way, their dreams had led them into **poverty** and **depression**.

She certainly did not want to be **stuck** with a depressingly low-paying job and a book that no one wanted to read. What an awful **fate** that would be. And so she decided to **throw** all her energy **into** starting a more **stable** career.

It would have to be a career where she could write every day, and immediately the idea of becoming a journalist seemed to be the most **feasible**. She knew she had the **academic** ability to study the trade and learn how to write news articles **professionally**. Her **intuition** proved to be right. The classes were no challenge for her. And she had the **discipline** to pursue the right **internship** she needed.

By the time she had graduated with her degree in **journalism**, Amy already had a job. She worked at a major **corporation** as an editor and **columnist**. Her **transition** into work life was **smooth**. And her parents were very proud of what she had achieved.

The hours were long, and the work was highly **demanding**. **Editing** news articles required careful thinking and **tough** decisions. Research was required as well and **time-consuming overall**. The **volume** of articles needing editing was extremely high, and Amy had to work fast to be able to **get** to all of them.

When it came to writing news stories, however, there was this immediate **sinking feeling** in her **gut**. The **format** given to her had a high number of **restrictions**. The corporation required information to be presented in such a way. And there was no room for her own ideas. It was simply researching certain facts and reporting them. **Essentially**, it was **grunt work**.

To be able to write her own style, she would have to be promoted to a **senior** columnist. And that could take up to 10 years to accomplish, she learned. The idea of doing this **constricted** style of writing for that long **sickened** her. Over time, these thoughts slowly turned into a growing **anxiety**. It made life **miserable** for Amy. As a result, she began to **resort to** alcohol to **ease** her pain.

The thought of having to wait 10 years to gain the freedom to write the way she wanted was just unbearable. She would be stuck **grinding away** at a job that **worked her to the bone**. On weekdays, Amy would come home so tired that she didn't want to do anything. All she wanted was to have a glass of wine and watch TV until it was time for bed. And on weekends, she would be too depressed to go out and do anything.

After **back-to-back** months of **unproductive** weekends, she went back to reading novels. Although this time, it wasn't the same. That **child-like fascination** she once had was no longer there.

There was this awful feeling **in the back of her mind** that made it quite difficult to focus on the story. It was **heartbreaking** to start to lose interest in something she was absolutely **mesmerized** by as a kid.

Why couldn't she go back to **simpler times**, when she could spend hours reading novels while dreaming about her own characters? Amy decided long ago that it was much too **risky** for her to start writing a novel. She knew the **slim** chances of it becoming successful.

But now, the idea was more exciting than it had ever been. The small possibility of it becoming a **best-seller brought out** strong feelings of joy she hadn't felt in quite some time. And even if the novel wasn't highly successful, she at least had to try. If she didn't, she knew that she would be **miserable** and eventually **bitter** as she got older.

Working as a corporate journalist was draining all the strength and **vitality** she needed to **pour into** her passion. The truth was clear. She would have to quit her high-paying job to **free** herself completely. The novel she always wanted to write would take forever to complete if she was just writing on the weekends. And even then, she would be writing while still exhausted from being **overworked** during the week. The writing would have to be done every day.

And so, Amy quit her **lucrative** journalist **position**. She then found part-time work as a **freelance** editor. It was a **severe** pay cut, but it was well worth having the time and energy to work every day on her dream.

It's difficult to say if she will **secure** a **publishing** deal or not. At this point, however, it no longer matters to Amy. **Peace of mind** is the only **guarantee**.

Vocabulary and Grammar

- **destined** --- having a future that has already been decided
- **magnetic** *(people)* --- attractive to people
- **draw (into)** *(attract)* --- to attract
- **devour** *(read)* --- to read sth. quickly and with great interest
- **investment** *(future)* --- sth. you buy because it will be useful later
- **relatively** --- very *(when compared to other things or people)*
- **pay off** *(succeed)* --- to bring good results and be successful
- **go unrecognized** --- to not be noticed or seen as important
- **obsession** --- something or sb. you think about all the time
- **intellect** --- the ability to think and understand things
- **objection** --- saying that you are against sth. or a reason for why
- **gifted** --- having a lot of intelligence or natural ability
- **a shame** --- used to say you are disappointed about sth.
- **escalate** --- to (make something) get worse or increase fast
- **straight A's** --- the highest grades in all your classes
- **recall** --- to remember
- **crack a joke** --- to make a joke
- **straight-up** --- honest(ly) and real(ly)
- **cleverly** --- in a way that is smart and effective
- **disguise** *[verb]* --- to change sth.'s image so it can't be recognized

For All the Wrong Reasons

- **indirect** *(hidden)* --- not done in a way that is clear and obvious
- **schooling** --- education received in school
- **pick up** *(start again)* --- to continue
- **reward** *[verb]* --- to give sth. good to sb. for doing sth. good
- **expectation** --- a belief that something will or should happen
- **fly** *(move quickly)* --- to go or move quickly
- **race against the clock** *[verb]* --- to finish sth. fast before it's too late
- **immerse** *(involve)* --- to become completely involved in sth.
- **complexity** --- having many parts and being hard to understand
- **there is sth. about** --- used to say sth. has an unknown quality to it
- **align** *(be similar)* --- to be similar or the same as sth. else
- **reveal** *(show)* --- to show something that had been hidden before
- **fascinate** --- to interest somebody very much
- **prove** *(show)* --- to show a particular result over time
- **push** *(persuade)* --- to persuade
- **freedom** *(power)* --- the power to do whatever you want
- **dorm** *(building)* --- a building for college students to live in
- **socialize** *(talk)* --- to spend time with other people for pleasure
- **party animal** --- a person who loves parties
- **genius** *(person)* --- sb. who is extremely intelligent, skilled, or creative
- **entrepreneur** --- someone who starts their own business

- **be in the same boat** --- to be in the same difficult situation
- **float around** *[idiom]* --- to not be in any exact place
- **find your place** --- to find a job, purpose, or passion that fits you
- **make it big** --- *(informal)* to become very successful or famous
- **pursue** *(try)* --- to try to do or achieve sth. over a period of time
- **land a deal** --- to successfully complete a big business agreement
- **turn down** --- to refuse a request or offer
- **dead-end job** --- a job where you can't get promoted
- **poverty** --- being extremely poor
- **depression** *(unhappiness)* --- deep sadness with a lack of hope
- **stuck** --- in a difficult situation that you cannot escape
- **fate** *(events)* --- what has happened or will happen to sb. or sth.
- **throw (yourself) into sth.** --- to begin to do sth. with great energy
- **stable** *(fixed)* --- not likely to change, move, or get worse
- **feasible** --- able and likely to be achieved
- **academic** *(education)* --- relating to education and studying
- **professionally** *(trained)* --- by a person who has been trained
- **intuition** --- the ability to understand sth. through just feeling
- **discipline** *(self)* --- the ability to control your own behavior
- **internship** *(student)* --- when a student works for experience at a job
- **journalism** --- the work of writing articles to tell news stories

For All the Wrong Reasons

- **corporation** --- a very large company or group of companies
- **columnist** --- a journalist who writes articles for a company
- **transition** --- the process of changing from one thing to another
- **smooth** *(process)* --- happening without problems
- **demanding** --- needing a lot of time and effort
- **edit** --- to make changes and correct mistakes in a text or film
- **tough** *(difficult)* --- hard
- **time-consuming** --- takes a lot of time
- **overall** --- (in) total or (in) general
- **volume** *(amount)* --- the amount of something
- **get** *(opportunity)* --- to have the chance to do something
- **sinking feeling** --- a feeling that sth. bad has happened or will happen
- **gut** *(feeling)* --- the part of a person that experiences emotions
- **format** *(arrangement)* --- the way something is arranged
- **restriction** --- a limit on something
- **essentially** --- when you think about the most important idea of sth.
- **grunt work** --- difficult, boring work
- **senior** *(rank)* --- high or higher in level inside a group of people
- **constricted** *(limited)* --- limited in some way(s)
- **sicken** *(disgust)* --- to make someone feel angry and shocked
- **anxiety** *(worry)* --- feeling nervous and worried that sth. bad will happen

- **miserable** *(unpleasant)* --- unpleasant and makes you unhappy
- **resort to** --- to do something you don't want to do to achieve sth.
- **ease** *(reduce)* --- to (make sth.) become less difficult, painful, etc.
- **grind away** --- to work hard
- **work sb. to the bone** --- to make sb. work very hard
- **back-to-back** *(continuous)* --- repeating without stopping
- **unproductive** --- producing little to no results that are good
- **child-like** --- having the good qualities that children have
- **fascination** --- when you feel extremely interested in something
- **in the back of your mind** --- in your thoughts but with no plan to do
- **heartbreaking** --- extremely sad
- **mesmerize** --- to hold the complete attention of somebody
- **simpler times** --- past days when you worried less and were happier
- **risky** --- having the possibility of something bad happening
- **slim** *(small)* --- very small
- **best-seller** --- a product that has sold a large number of copies
- **bring out something** *(appear)* --- to make something appear
- **miserable** *(unhappy)* --- very unhappy or uncomfortable
- **bitter** *(people)* --- angry and unhappy because of the past
- **vitality** *(energy)* --- energy and strength
- **pour into** --- to spend a lot of money or energy on something

- **free** *(make available)* --- to make sb. or sth. available for sth.
- **overworked** *(people)* --- made to work too much
- **lucrative** --- *(used for jobs and businesses)* making a lot of money
- **position** *(job)* --- a job
- **freelance** --- doing work for many companies rather than just one
- **severe** *(serious)* --- very serious or bad
- **secure** *(get)* --- *(formal)* to get sth. that is usually hard to get
- **publishing** --- preparing and selling books, magazines, games, etc.
- **peace of mind** --- a feeling of being calm and not worried at all
- **guarantee** *(promise)* --- a promise that sth. will be done or will happen

Comprehension Questions

1. Amy's parents saw their child's obsession with reading as...
    A) a sign of creativity.
    B) a sign of high intellect.
    C) a sign of hope.
    D) a sign from the gods.

2. What kind of pressure did Amy face while in high school?
    A) She was expected to read novels given to her by her father.
    B) She was expected to get the highest grades every semester.
    C) She was expected to perform her best every trimester.
    D) She was expected to take extra classes and quiz her mother.

3. How did Amy's mom disguise her intentions?
    A) With love and a silly character
    B) With cleverness and a stupid voice
    C) With love and a cartoon character
    D) With cleverness and a dumb voice

4. What was it about reading fiction that attracted Amy?
    A) Characters' actions didn't always match their public image.
    B) There was something about the alignment of actions.
    C) There was something about the complexity of the levels.
    D) There was something fascinating about revealing things.

5. What kind of people did Amy meet in college?
    A) Party animals, geniuses, entrepreneurs, and athletes
    B) Party animals, sorcerers, warriors, and rogues
    C) Party animals, students, boats, and floaters
    D) Party animals, authors, characters, and publishers

6. According to the story, why do most writers fail to find success?
    A) They cannot get out of poverty and depression.
    B) They pay the bills by working dead-end jobs.
    C) They float around trying to find their place in society.
    D) They cannot get a deal with a major publisher.

7. What were working conditions like for Amy at the corporation?
    A) It was a difficult job that required editing and volume.
    B) It was a tough job that required research and volume.
    C) It was a demanding job with a high volume of work.
    D) It was a piece of cake.

For All the Wrong Reasons

8. Why didn't Amy like writing as a journalist for the corporation?
    A) It was way too easy and didn't challenge her at all.
    B) The work became too political.
    C) There weren't enough office parties offering free food.
    D) There were too many restrictions imposed on her writing.

9. Amy would become miserable and bitter if she didn't do what?
    A) Stay young
    B) Drain all of her strength and vitality
    C) Try to write a best-selling novel
    D) Overwork herself

10. Why did Amy quit her job as a corporate journalist?
    A) She found a better paying job as a freelancer.
    B) She got a publishing deal for her new novel.
    C) She didn't quit. She got fired.
    D) She needed the time to focus on writing her novel.

CHAPTER THREE:

THE LESSER OF TWO EVILS

The American **presidential** election season was **underway**. Only one could be the next **commander-in-chief**. Many politicians had campaigned over the last two years, trying to gather enough support. But the competition was too strong for the **vast majority** and for good reason. After all, they were competing to become the "**leader of the free world.**"

For one reason or another, voters did not join their **cause**. Some had excellent policy ideas that were smart and practical, but their personalities were weak. Their words were carefully **rehearsed** and didn't sound **authentic** at all. If someone was going to become president, they would have to *seem* **genuine at heart**.

Yet most sounded like any other politician. They made the same promises voters have heard hundreds of times in the past. If they were **elected**, they would create jobs, work hard for the **middle class**, and invest in education. It was the same old **rhetoric** heard again and again. And the people **were sick of it**.

Other candidates **stood out** a little too much. **Scandals** are a part of every election cycle, and just one could **doom** any politician's career. Sex scandals, in particular, were a political **death sentence**. News of **affairs** was common, but sometimes the details got quite **disturbing**. This year, one candidate was caught on camera **inappropriately** touching **underaged** girls at a public event. The news media quickly learned of the event. Soon, news stories **speculating** that the man was a **pedophile** were on TV all day and night. From that point, it **was only a matter of time** until he **dropped out**.

Even if candidates seemed like they were good people, ones who were mentally slow were **humiliated** and then **eliminated** as well. A candidate could be very **well spoken** 99% of the time, but sometimes all it **takes** is just one mistake to end someone's campaign. Anything said in front of a camera can be shared and **played back infinitely**. This can be used to destroy someone's **reputation**, even one built across decades.

Some of these mistakes can be forgiven, yet there is one that cannot. And that is **corruption**. But unfortunately, it's very hard to prove how corrupt any **given** politician is. This is because so much takes place **behind closed doors** in Washington. Who knows what kind of **shady** deals are made during secret meetings with the rich and powerful? When politicians need to raise more money than their competitors to win elections, sacrifices must be made.

Here is when the **slippery slope** begins. How many **morals** is someone willing to sacrifice to win the **race**? How many **lobbyists** will they meet and take money from in exchange for political favors? How many of these political favors will hurt the public? And how much will they hurt?

Because corporations and **billionaires** invest millions of dollars into candidates, it's difficult to say where a politician's true **loyalties** lie. They may become fully **compromised**. They may even reach a **state** where every public statement they make is completely controlled. At that point, they are essentially bought and paid for. They are **puppets**.

The result of this system are politicians that seem **fake** and not at all authentic. They study, research, and train themselves to be a public image that **appeals** to the most amount of people. But voters **see** right **through** it. Some, however, are better actors.

In the end, every race almost always **comes down to** two candidates, one from each major political party. The-two party system makes sure of this. But what kind of people are actually able to secure these two **spots**? Surely, they would be the most appealing and **charming** choices. But sadly, no, at least not in recent years. Many popular candidates fail to gather enough money and support to stay in the race. Other times, one party would pour all of its resources into one candidate and quickly **annihilate** all other candidates in the party.

And so the country must often choose between two corrupt and compromised individuals. This is true for the presidential but also **congressional** and local elections. Of course, it is the presidential election that receives the most attention. So what two choices have Americans been given for president this year?

First, there is the **liberal** candidate Robert Hamilton. His **lovable** personality and charming behavior makes it easy to understand the appeal he has with many voters. He's incredibly nice to every reporter, politician, and **citizen** he comes across.

Upon further **inspection**, however, it's obvious his policies are very **vague** with no real meaning behind them. Look at anytime Hamilton is **thoroughly** questioned about his economic policies, for example. There comes a point where he will crack a joke and quickly change topics. His charm, great **timing**, and quick **wit** make it work so well. He has **mastered** the **art** of giving an answer that sounds nice but doesn't answer the question at all.

And second, the **conservative** candidate, Jeffery Copperfield, is not all that much better. He's a master salesman who knows how to sell people on an idea. His team has created simple yet powerful campaign **slogans** that promise real change. It's difficult to say how well he will **deliver** on his **revolutionary** ideas if he's elected.

Unfortunately, Copperfield has a reputation for having a **big mouth** and also lying. When questioned about his past statements by reporters, he responds with a **verbal attack**. He's **ruthless** with his **insults**. And he doesn't **hold back**.

His aim is to destroy their **credibility** as sources of news. It's part of his **strategy** to get people to question the **integrity** of the liberal media. That way they will vote **anti**-liberal.

Given his **popularity**, it has been most definitely effective. Now the media appears to be mainly focusing on just attacking him rather than doing their job of delivering the news. This has **swayed** more voters to his side.

Hamilton and Copperfield are now **neck and neck** in the **polls**. **Regardless** of who wins, it seems the country loses either way. Corporations and billionaires will win, but the people will lose. With choices like these, it makes sense why some people don't vote at all. **Damned if they do, damned if they don't**.

Throughout history, when a political system becomes corrupted and broken, the people **rise up** and start a **revolution**. **Starvation** and **injustice** are the usual starting points. But what happens when the people are given **unlimited** food and entertainment for a very cheap price like in America today? How long can people **bury** their problems before something has to change? What will be the final straw?

Vocabulary and Grammar

- **the lesser of two evils** --- the less terrible of two terrible choices
- **presidential** --- connected to a president
- **underway** --- happening now
- **commander-in-chief** --- the head of a state or an army
- **vast** --- extremely large
- **majority** *(largest)* --- the largest part of something
- **leader of the free world** --- (the president of) the United States
- **for one reason or another** --- for all sorts of reasons
- **cause** *(idea)* --- an idea that people support or fight for
- **rehearse** *(speech)* --- to practice sth. you want to say in the future
- **authentic** --- real or is really what somebody says it is
- **genuine** *(person)* --- honest
- **at heart** --- used to say what someone really is
- **elect** --- to choose someone for a job by voting
- **middle class** --- people who are not very rich or poor
- **rhetoric** --- language used to influence people (that isn't honest)
- **be sick of something** --- to be bored or annoyed by something
- **stand out** *(be noticed)* --- to be easily noticed
- **scandal** *(event)* --- an event that makes people shocked and angry
- **doom** *[verb]* --- to make sth. extremely bad certain to happen

The Lesser of Two Evils

- **death sentence** (*event*) --- an event that ends something forever
- **affair** (*relationship*) --- a secret sexual relationship
- **disturbing** --- making you feel upset or anxious
- **inappropriately** --- in a way that is wrong in a particular situation
- **underaged** --- younger than the age when something is allowed
- **speculate** (*guess*) --- to guess without knowing all the facts
- **pedophile** --- a person who is sexually attracted to children
- **be only a matter of time** --- used to say sth. will happen in the future
- **drop out** (*activity*) --- to decide to no longer be involved with sth.
- **humiliate** --- to make somebody feel stupid or ashamed
- **eliminate** --- to defeat sb. so that they're removed from a competition
- **well spoken** --- speaking in a way that is educated and pleasant
- **take** (*need*) --- to need or require
- **play back** --- to play something that has been recorded
- **infinitely** --- very much or without limit
- **reputation** --- the general opinion people have about sb. or sth.
- **corruption** (*behavior*) --- illegal behavior by people in power
- **given** [*adjective*] --- particular
- **behind closed doors** --- without the public knowing
- **shady** (*illegal*) --- illegal or not honest
- **slippery slope** --- a bad habit that is difficult to stop once it starts

- **morals** *(beliefs)* --- beliefs of what is good and bad behavior
- **race** *(politics)* --- a competition for political power
- **lobbyist** --- a person whose job is to influence politicians
- **billionaire** --- a person who has at least $1,000,000,000
- **loyalty** *(feeling)* --- a strong feeling of support for sb. or sth.
- **compromised** *(person)* --- not acting honestly or with good intentions
- **state** *(condition)* --- condition
- **puppet** *(person)* --- sb. whose actions are controlled by sb. else
- **fake** *[adjective]* --- not real but looks real
- **appeal** *(interest)* --- to interest or attract someone
- **see through** --- to realize someone is tricking you
- **come down to** --- to depend on a single most important point
- **spot** *(competition)* --- a place in a competition, team, or event
- **charming** *(attractive)* --- very attractive and pleasant
- **annihilate** --- to destroy something or defeat completely
- **congressional** --- relating to a national group of elected politicians
- **liberal** *(US)* --- (sb.) supporting social services and change
- **lovable** --- easy to love
- **citizen** *(country)* --- a legal member of a particular country
- **inspection** *(act)* --- the act of looking at sth. closely
- **vague** *(details)* --- not giving enough information about sth.

- **thoroughly** *(carefully)* --- in a careful and detailed way
- **timing** *(skill)* --- the skill of doing sth. exactly at the right time
- **wit** *(ability)* --- the ability to use words in a clever and funny way
- **master** *(learn)* --- to learn something completely
- **art** *(skill)* --- skill built through study, practice, and experience
- **conservative** *(US)* --- (sb.) supporting tradition and responsibility
- **slogan** --- a short, easily remembered phrase used to advertise sth.
- **deliver** *(produce)* --- to produce something that was promised
- **revolutionary** *(change)* --- causing a complete change
- **big mouth** --- someone who has a big mouth talks too much
- **verbal** *(spoken)* --- spoken
- **attack** *(criticism)* --- a very strong criticism of sb. or sth.
- **ruthless** --- not caring about hurting others at all
- **insult** --- something said or done that is rude to make sb. upset
- **hold back** *(not do)* --- to (make somebody) not say or do sth.
- **credibility** --- the quality of being believed and trusted
- **strategy** --- a large plan made of many smaller plans
- **integrity** *(honesty)* --- honesty and ability to do the right thing
- **anti-** --- against *(disagree with)*
- **popularity** --- the quality of being liked by many people
- **sway** *(persuade)* --- to persuade or influence

- **neck and neck** --- having the same score in a competition
- **poll** --- questioning many people about their opinion about sth.
- **regardless** --- despite the current situation
- **damned if you do, damned if you don't** --- either choice will be bad
- **rise up** --- to fight against your government, leader, or an enemy
- **revolution** *(politics)* --- a complete change to a government by force
- **starvation** --- suffering or dying from a lack of food
- **injustice** --- a situation or act being completely unfair
- **unlimited** --- not limited
- **bury** *(forget)* --- to try to forget a bad feeling or experience

Comprehension Questions

1. Presidential candidates are NOT competing to become...
    A) the lesser of two evils.
    B) the commander-in-chief.
    C) the president of the United States.
    D) the leader of the free world.

2. The story mentions that voters were tired of hearing what?
    A) The loud music at rallies
    B) The sound of debating politicians
    C) The same old promises from politicians
    D) The non-stop news coverage of the election

3. What actual scandal was caught on camera?
    A) An affair
    B) A candidate awkwardly touching teenage girls
    C) The dooming and death sentencing of a politician's career
    D) A public event

4. What is the one mistake that cannot be forgiven in the story?
    A) Corruption
    B) Scandals
    C) Incompetence
    D) Wordiness

5. What does it mean if a politician is fully compromised?
    A) They buy and pay for lobbyists.
    B) They control every public statement they make.
    C) They have invested millions of dollars into a candidate.
    D) They are loyal to the rich and powerful but not the people.

6. What does it mean if someone is fake?
    A) They are a politician.
    B) Their personality is not authentic.
    C) They appear to be what they really are.
    D) They study and research people.

7. If you have a charming and lovable personality, ...
    A) you are incredibly nice, and people like you.
    B) you are fairly rude, and people don't like you.
    C) you are very lucky, and good things happen to you.
    D) you are largely unlucky, and bad things happen to you.

8. Robert Hamilton does what when questioned about his policy?
    A) He gives a proper explanation of his policy.
    B) He cracks a joke and comes to a point.
    C) He changes the subject using charm and wit.
    D) He masters the art of answering questions.

9. What does Jeffery Copperfield do when reporters question him about his past statements?
    A) He physically attacks and harms them.
    B) He verbally attacks and insults them.
    C) He mentally attacks and confuses them.
    D) He psychologically attacks and tortures them.

10. According to the story, who is currently leading in the polls?
    A) Hamilton
    B) Copperfield
    C) It's a tie between liberals and conservatives.
    D) It's a tie between Hamilton and Copperfield.

CHAPTER FOUR:

THE RISE OF THE INFLUENCER

Michael had just earned his first million dollars. His friends and family were in **disbelief**. Just a few years ago, many of them were **doubtful** he was going to **get anywhere** with the business he had started. **In their eyes**, Michael had made a series of odd choices throughout his life, and this was just another of his crazy ideas.

Now, however, his **peers** were calling him a genius! How else could he have had this much success? Only geniuses come up with ideas that make that much money.

Although, if we examine Michael's life a little more closely, what made him rich will become more **apparent**. There were certain beliefs and **mindsets** he **adopted** that eventually grew into financial success. They were ideas and ways of thinking that anyone could use if they chose to focus on them. In other words, anyone could achieve what Michael had.

Early in life, Michael started out with very few **gifts**. He was a **mediocre** student who didn't care much for school. He was the **class clown** and was more interested in getting a laugh than getting a good grade. For years, teachers and **counselors** warned him. They told him that if he continued down this **path**, he was going to have to face the consequences of his actions. And of course, Michael didn't listen.

They wanted him gone from their classrooms. So they all gave him low but **barely** passing grades just so he would not have to repeat their classes. On his graduation day, it was almost as if all of his teachers gave him a **sarcastic** look. It was a look that said, "Congratulations. Now get out."

Michael spent the first years of his adult life **jumping** from job to job. He worked at **retail stores**, restaurants, factories, and even as a **janitor**. They all taught him how to work hard, deal with people, and act like an adult. Earning his own money and becoming independent from his parents was at first challenging. But eventually, it became a **liberating** experience.

In his early **twenties**, Michael was always able to find work yet only for dead-end jobs. **Living paycheck to paycheck**, he was unable to save any money. He had no special talents to share with the world. His life was going nowhere, and it scared him **deeply**.

Then one day, while he was working in sales, he had a thought. He wondered why some of his **co-workers** were making so much more than he was. They were in the office working for **roughly** the same amount of time he was. Yet they were able to make thousands more in sales than him. What were they doing differently, he asked himself.

These **burning questions** kept bothering him day after day. That was until he decided to ask the highest earning salesman directly. The man said to him that there was a book out there that changed his life. If he wanted to make more sales, that book would definitely help him, he was told.

He was **intrigued** by the idea that a book could change his life. So Michael bought a copy and began reading it immediately. While he was a poor student in school, he was not **illiterate**. Even reading at a slow **pace**, he was determined to **power through** the whole book.

He was fascinated by the author's message of **self-mastery**. He even grabbed a pen and some paper and began to take notes while reading. The author told stories about some of the most successful people who ever lived and explained what made each of them so brilliant at their **craft**. These were stories about men and women who **overcame obstacles** that seemed impossible. But somehow and some way they were able to **break through**. In each story, a person from history came across a very important lesson during their life. It would prove to be a lesson that completely **altered** the **course** of their lives.

By the time Michael had finished the book, he was filled with **determination** and hope for the future. He realized that he was completely responsible for himself. If he wanted to change his life situation, he had to change his environment and everything he allowed inside his mind and body.

This meant changing what time meant to him and how it should be spent. He had to change what media he watched, read, and listened to. He had to change his entertainment to something that **empowered** him with **creativity**. He even had to change what foods he ate to give him the necessary **fuel** to get more done each and every day.

Time was his most valuable resource of all, he learned. Time spent watching TV and movies was giving Michael zero **return** on his **investment**. Entertainment that provided only **short-term** pleasure was no longer an acceptable use of his time. It was much **wiser** to invest it **elsewhere**.

Soon, his mornings started with **audiobooks** instead of checking his smartphone. His afternoons were opportunities to learn new skills, like video editing and **public speaking**. And his evenings were spent relaxing, watching educational videos, and listening to **informative** podcasts. Everything he did was a step towards his goals.

Michael also started investing money into himself. He stopped spending his paychecks on video games, alcohol, and eating out all the time. Instead, he bought several books on the art of selling.

His **mission** was to **figure out** the best sales strategies he could immediately use. The goal was to quickly increase his **revenue**.

And he succeeded. Within a year, he was able to **triple** the amount of products he sold to customers. As a result, he had tripled his own **income**.

And things only continued to grow. After about a year of studying by himself, Michael had **accumulated** a lot of knowledge and a couple of new skills. But what would he do with what he had learned? He was quickly rising to the top of the sales team at his company, so he now started to feel he was **capable** of something far more **ambitious**.

After many months of careful thinking, he decided to become a **motivational speaker**. The past year had proved to him how a message of **encouragement** could change someone's life. It certainly had changed his.

His family had grown up poor, not just in terms of money but thinking too. Whenever things did not **go their way**, his parents would complain. They blamed other people for their problems. Sometimes this included Michael. This was how they dealt with their **anger** and **frustration**.

Work was something to suffer through in order to pay the bills and barely **get by**. Any extra money was spent on immediate pleasures, like eating out at restaurants or buying expensive clothing. No money was ever saved. It was this kind of thinking Michael had **inherited** from his mom and dad.

But now he knew much better. He wanted to show the world how to think rich. Not everyone wants to be rich, of course. But he would teach how someone's way of thinking could make them poor or rich, both **financially** *and* mentally. The goal was to **inspire** people to do and achieve things they never thought they would be capable of.

His message would be his own story. It would be the story of how he was once a **nobody going nowhere** with his life. And then, somehow he **turned it all around**. It would be an example of how to go from being a **broke D student** in high school to being successful and in complete control of your life. It would be his **zero to hero** story.

Michael would use his **newly acquired** video editing and public speaking skills to create content on social media. Unfortunately, it was slow to gain any real **following** in its first year. He, however, did not look for things to blame for the slow start. Instead, he made it his mission to figure out what he could do to grow his influence. He was committed to a life of constant learning, and succeeding at social media was another thing he would learn.

To make his videos more appealing to viewers, he **utilized** the power of attractive titles and **thumbnails**. Sure, accurate titles and thumbnails properly describe videos, but they draw little to no attention. Good titles **provoke** people. They make **bold** statements. They make people think, "Well, now I have to find out if that's true or not."

Content was the other essential **component** he needed to master. Videos of himself in his living room just talking into the camera weren't performing very well. He had to increase his **production value**. Michael began filming videos from **multiple** cameras and locations. And in the editing process, he combined his video **footage** with images and **animation**. With these improvements and his **witty** personality, he was able to make something incredible and **inspirational**.

His second year on social media **landed** him enormous success. The newer videos **resonated** with what people were feeling. They were **compelled** to share them with their family, friends, and followers. Those people then shared the videos with their own family, friends, and followers, causing a cycle. As a result, many of his videos went **viral**. They were making thousands of dollars in ad revenue, and he was gaining hundreds of thousands of fans.

Because of his popularity and skills as a public speaker, he was invited and paid to speak at large events. Here he gained even more money and **fame**. At these events, he also met a large number of other content **creators**. Many of **whom** wanted to **collaborate** with him. By the end, he returned home with a long list of contacts who were not only super creative but super friendly as well.

His success continued to **snowball**. With his huge and still growing social media following, Michael **launched** his own **line** of **merchandise**. He sold mugs, shirts, and **hoodies** all with his popular **catchphrases** on them. There were also many **sponsorship** deals he was offered, but he only accepted those for products he actually used. They were products he believed in like health supplements and educational tools. And finally, he even did **live streams** where he took **donations** from fans and answered their questions.

By his third year on social media, he realized he had more money that he would ever need in his life. Michael had become financially independent for the rest of his life.

The former class clown with no future was now **wealthy**. His family and friends were **dumbfounded**. How could someone like that become rich? It had to have been luck. If not luck, it was because he had a natural talent for being funny. There was just no other way they could accept it. But Michael knew it was more than luck and talent that allowed him to reach this point.

The greatest reward, however, was neither the wealth nor the fame but the person he had become. If there was something he **truly** wanted, he would allow nothing to get between him and his goal. He had become the **unstoppable** force.

With this power and wealth, he would not retire and live a life of luxury with fancy houses, clothes, and parties. No. That would be far too boring. Now was the time to find the next thing he would build. And this time, it would be bigger than himself.

Vocabulary and Grammar

- **rise** *(process)* --- the process of becoming more powerful or popular

- **influencer (online)** --- sb. who is paid to promote products on social media

- **disbelief** --- the feeling of not believing something is true

- **doubtful** --- not sure or not likely

- **get anywhere** --- to make any progress

- **in somebody's eyes** --- in somebody's opinion

- **peer** *(equal)* --- sb. who is in the same situation as you in society

- **apparent** *(obvious)* --- easy to see or understand

- **mindset** --- a way of thinking someone has that is hard to change

- **adopt** *(method)* --- to start using a new method

- **gift** *(ability)* --- a special ability or talent

- **mediocre** --- not good enough
- **class clown** --- a student who makes jokes a lot during class
- **counselor** *(advice)* --- sb. who listens and gives advice to sb. as a job
- **path** *(actions)* --- a set of actions in life or achieving something
- **barely** --- by a very small amount
- **sarcastic** --- using words that are the opposite of what you mean
- **jump (change)** --- to change
- **retail store** --- a store that sells products to the public
- **janitor** --- a person whose job is to clean and take care of a building
- **liberating** --- making you feel you are free from anyone's control
- **twenties** --- the time when you are between 20 and 29 years old
- **live paycheck to paycheck** --- to spend all the money you earn
- **deeply** *(very)* --- very (much)
- **co-worker** --- a person you work with
- **roughly** *(about)* --- approximately
- **burning question** --- a question that must be answered quickly
- **intrigue** --- to make somebody very interested
- **illiterate** --- unable to read and write
- **pace** *(speed)* --- the speed at which something moves or happens
- **power through** --- to continue until the end of sth. difficult
- **self-mastery** --- the ability to control your feelings and life

The Rise of the Influencer

- **craft** *(job)* --- a job or activity where skill is needed
- **overcome** *(succeed)* --- to succeed in dealing with a problem
- **obstacle** --- sth. that blocks you and slows movement or action
- **break through** *(achieve)* --- to achieve success despite problems
- **alter** *(change)* --- to change
- **course** *(development)* --- the way which something develops
- **determination** *(ability)* --- the ability to continue doing sth. hard
- **empower** *(support)* --- to give someone the power to achieve sth.
- **creativity** --- the ability to make something original
- **fuel** *(food)* --- food, drink, or drugs that give energy
- **return** *(profit)* --- the profit you make on something you invest in
- **investment** --- the act of investing money, time or effort into sth.
- **short-term** --- lasting or relating to a short period of time
- **wise** --- sensible or having the ability to make good decisions
- **elsewhere** --- to, in, or at another place or other places
- **audiobook** --- recorded books you listen to
- **public speaking** --- the act of speaking on a topic to a group of people
- **informative** --- giving a lot of useful information
- **mission** *(personal)* --- work that you feel it is your duty to do
- **figure out** --- to think about sb. or sth. until you finally understand it
- **revenue** --- the money a government or a business receives

- **triple** *[verb]* --- to (make sth.) increase by three times
- **income** --- money that is earned from work, business, or investing
- **accumulate** *(collect)* --- to slowly collect more of sth. over time
- **capable** *(able)* --- having the skills and abilities to do something
- **ambitious** *(thing)* --- needing a lot of effort to succeed
- **motivational speaker** --- sb. whose job is to give encouraging speeches
- **encouragement** --- words or actions that give confidence or hope
- **go somebody's way** --- to happen in a way that somebody likes
- **anger** *[noun]* --- an angry feeling
- **frustration** *(feeling)* --- an angry feeling you get when you can't do sth.
- **get by** --- to manage to live or do sth. with the little you have
- **inherit** *(belief)* --- to have a belief you got from your family
- **financially** --- in a way that is connected to money or how it is managed
- **inspire** *(encourage)* --- to make sb. feel they want to and can do sth.
- **nobody** *[noun]* --- a person who is not important
- **go nowhere** --- to make no progress
- **turn sth. around** --- to change sth. unsuccessful into a success
- **broke** *(money)* --- having no money
- **D student** --- a student who gets very low grades *(D's)* in school
- **zero to hero** --- a situation where sb. goes from unsuccessful to successful
- **newly** --- recently

The Rise of the Influencer

- **acquire** *(skill)* --- to gain new knowledge or a new skill
- **following** *(people)* --- a group of people who support sb. or sth.
- **utilize** --- *(formal)* to use
- **thumbnail** *(computer)* --- a small image on a computer screen
- **provoke** *(cause)* --- to cause a (negative) reaction in someone
- **bold** *(confident)* --- confident and not afraid
- **component** --- one of many parts in which something is made
- **production value** --- the quality of art in terms of money spent
- **multiple** --- many
- **footage** *(film)* --- film of a particular event
- **animation** *(process)* --- the process of creating moving images
- **witty** --- clever and funny
- **inspirational** --- making sb. feel they want to and can do sth.
- **land** *(get)* --- to succeed in getting something you wanted
- **resonate** *(similar)* --- to be similar to what sb. thinks or believes
- **compel** *(necessary)* --- to make doing something necessary
- **viral** *(internet)* --- very popular and shared a lot on the internet
- **fame** --- being famous
- **creator** --- someone who has created something
- **whom** --- used instead of 'who' as the object of a verb or preposition
- **collaborate** *(create)* --- to work with sb. to create or achieve sth.

- **snowball** *[verb]* --- to quickly grow and become more important
- **launch** *(product)* --- to start selling a product to the public
- **line** *(product)* --- a set of products that a company makes
- **merchandise** --- goods that are bought and sold
- **hoody** --- a sweatshirt with a hood *(a part that covers your head)*
- **catchphrase** --- a popular phrase that is connected to sb. famous
- **sponsorship** --- money given to sb. to support them or to advertise sth.
- **live stream** *[noun]* --- a live video with sound of sth. over the internet
- **donation** *(money)* --- money or goods given to people to help them
- **wealthy** --- very rich
- **dumbfounded** --- so surprised you cannot speak
- **truly** --- real(ly)
- **unstoppable** --- unable to be stopped

The Rise of the Influencer

Comprehension Questions

1. In whose eyes did Michael's business ideas seem crazy?
    A) Geniuses and his peers'
    B) His eyes
    C) His family and friends'
    D) Nobody's eyes

2. What kind of student was Michael in school?
    A) He was the straight A student.
    B) He was gifted.
    C) He was creative and sarcastic.
    D) He was mediocre and the class clown.

3. At which of the following places did Michael not work?
    A) Factories
    B) Retail stores
    C) Restaurants
    D) He worked at all of the above.

4. In the story, Michael has multiple burning questions at one point. Which of the following was one of them?
    A) Which book would change his life?
    B) How were his co-workers making more time than him?
    C) What were the other salesmen doing differently than him?
    D) How should I ask the highest earning salesman?

5. How did Michael feel after reading the book suggested to him?
    A) He wanted to write his own book.
    B) He was filled with anger and disgust.
    C) He became empowered and hopeful for the future.
    D) He was determined to change the environment.

6. How did Michael invest money into himself?
    A) He bought books about selling.
    B) He spent his paychecks on video games, alcohol, and food.
    C) He tripled the sales he made and his own income.
    D) He watched educational videos.

7. Acting as a clown during school helped Michael cope with what?
    A) His ability to deal with his own anger and frustration
    B) His messages of encouragement
    C) His parents' complaints and anger issues
    D) His lack of inheritance

8. What story did Michael tell in his videos?
    A) The history of inspiration and capability
    B) The story of a D student who became an A student
    C) The story of a hero who turned into a zero
    D) The story of a loser who turned his life around

9. How did Michael grow his YouTube channel?
    A) He improved his titles, thumbnails, and video content.
    B) He mainly collaborated with other content creators.
    C) He provoked people by using bold statements.
    D) He used multiple cameras, crews, locations.

10. How do influencers make their money?
    A) Through sponsorships, ad revenue, and merchandise
    B) Through live streams, hoodies, and catchphrases
    C) Through shirts, donations, and snowballs
    D) All of the above

CHAPTER FIVE:

BIG FISH

Rhonda was what you might call an **overachiever**. A very competitive **spirit** was at her **core**. And she was always on the **hunt** for more. It was a hunt to learn more, achieve more, do more, win more, and be more.

In school, she was the big fish in the small pond. She was brought up to treat her classmates with respect and a friendly attitude. But when it was test time, they all became **minnows** to feed her **insatiable** desire to be the best. With **relative ease**, she graduated as the top of her class.

Boys were drawn to her large, **emerald** eyes and their powerful **stare**. Her look was **hypnotic**. And when she got older, her **innocent** face and **subtle** features could and did attract a long line of men ready to marry her, if she wanted. But she did not desire the life of a simple housewife. She knew she could be more, so much more.

At university, Rhonda **met her match intellectually**. There were folks **raised** from birth to become lawyers and doctors at her school. Try as she did, she would go neck and neck with some of the best **brains** in the country, until a certain point, that is.

After chatting with her peers, she learned that some of them were **putting in** a **fraction** of the study time and effort she was. And they got higher scores than her. She couldn't believe it. **Her heart sank**. How could she compete with those who **effortlessly** did better than her best effort? Defeat was **undeniable**.

Her interest in school **vanished** almost completely. There was no point in trying anymore. Her energy had vanished, too. She became depressed for a few weeks. Life had made sense until this point. Who was she at this point, she asked. She was a nobody, she answered.

It was through sports that she found new life for her competitive spirit. Rhonda **was** neither the fastest nor **one for** teamwork. But she was willing to **go to lengths** that not many other girls would. And so she took up **weightlifting**.

In a sport **dominated** by men, she definitely **stood out** from the crowd. Being a woman meant a slow start and a **pitiful foundation** for upper body strength. But over time her advantages were revealed. With enough **reps** and **sets**, she learned her legs were quite strong. Having a diet full of good **nutrition** and lots of **protein** helped her legs grow.

Learning about proper lifting and training techniques was also important. It allowed her to safely add increasing amounts of weight, reps, and **intensity** during workouts. The result was a cycle of her becoming stronger and stronger and lifting heavier and heavier **loads**. And all the extra muscle would go mostly to her lower body. This allowed her to maintain her cute upper **frame**.

Going to the gym, lifting, and getting stronger became her life. She could only make limited **gains** on the upper body lifts like the **bench press**. But Rhonda was **breaking** personal records for lower body lifts week after week. The progress was addicting. For years, she trained and **pushed** her body to its limits. Soon enough, she easily had the strongest **squat** and **deadlift** at her local gym, men included too.

It was time to **put** her strength **to the test**. She entered a local **powerlifting** competition intending to **go all out**. The months of training **leading up to** the event were extremely challenging. These training sessions were some of the most **sadistic** workouts she had ever **endured**. But she went to bed each night sore, knowing she put in as much work as she possibly could.

The day of the **meet** and competition had come, and it had gone. Rhonda was awarded 1st place after a serious battle with some tough competition in her weight **class**. She barely **squeaked** by with a **victory** against some of the strongest women out there. She even **put up** some **respectable** numbers compared to the men.

But something happened that night deep inside Rhonda. The obvious **move** now was to go and **seek** larger competition. There she was supposed to train even harder. Her **aspirations** should be **potentially** competing in the Olympics or starting a business like a gym or a line of supplements.

But suddenly she didn't want any of that. Rhonda didn't want or feel anything **for that matter**. She felt nothing, and it **terrified** her. For the first time in her life, the big fish had no **hunger**. The hunger for more had been the **driving force** of her life. And now, she was without it and without life.

A **dark** depression once again **took hold** of her. But this time, it was different. It was **self-destructive**. She started drinking heavily just to remember what it was like to feel joy or even anything again. She drank so much that her body stopped **craving** food **altogether**. It only craved alcohol.

Rhonda did not desire death, however. A year of time had allowed her to **process** the **emptiness** and despair she experienced. Perhaps she was not **destined** to be an **all-star** student. Nor was she destined to be a **world-class** athlete. But it no longer mattered. **For once**, she was **content** with the idea of being normal.

A **realization** had occurred in her mind. She saw that people are **beings** of **infinite potential** and imagination. But there is a limit to people's ability to care. At some point, things no longer matter. In the end, nothing really matters. And Rhonda was OK with that. It brought her peace.

Slowly but surely, her drinking **subsided** and plans for a bright future returned. She was now on a **quest** to find **fulfillment**. This time it would be in a more **modest** lifestyle.

Why was she was so competitive **in the first place**? If she could **tap into** that energy, she could use it to do or make something to help other people. The answers would not come easy. They would take time. They would take years.

Maybe even one day that hunger would return once more. And if it did, she would be ready.

Vocabulary and Grammar

- **big fish (in a small pond)** --- sb. important (but only in a small group)

- **overachiever** --- sb. who achieves more than is expected of them

- **spirit** *(person)* --- a person

- **core** *(main part)* --- the most important or basic part of sth.

- **hunt** *(search)* --- a search for something or sb. that is hard to find

- **minnow** *(person)* --- an unimportant person or group

- **insatiable** --- always wanting more of something

- **relative** *(if compared)* --- true if compared to other things

Big Fish

- **ease** *(no difficulty)* --- lack of difficulty
- **emerald** *[adjective]* --- bright green
- **stare** *[noun]* --- a long look at someone or something
- **hypnotic** *(attracting)* --- holding your attention like magic
- **innocent** *(young)* --- having little experience of the bad things in life
- **subtle** *(important)* --- small but important
- **meet your match** --- to meet sb. equal to or better than you at sth.
- **intellectually** --- in a way that involves thinking and understanding
- **raise** *(child)* --- to take care of a child until they become an adult
- **brain** *(person)* --- an intelligent person
- **put sth. in** *(time)* --- to spend a lot of time and effort doing sth.
- **fraction** *(part)* --- a small part or amount of something
- **sb.'s heart sinks** --- used to say sb. feels very sad about something
- **effortlessly** --- in a way that does not need effort
- **undeniable** --- certain or true
- **vanish** --- to disappear suddenly
- **be one for something** --- to like something
- **go to lengths** --- to try very hard to achieve something
- **weightlifting** --- lifting heavy weights as a sport or for exercise
- **dominate** *(be largest)* --- to be the largest or most important part of sth.
- **stand out** *(be seen)* --- to be very easily seen

- **pitiful** *(bad)* --- extremely bad
- **foundation** *(part)* --- the most basic part of sth. from which it grows
- **rep** *(exercise)* --- a short, single movement that is done many times
- **set** *(exercise)* --- a group of reps done without stopping
- **nutrition** *(food)* --- food that is needed to be strong and healthy
- **protein** --- a substance found in meat, eggs, beans, peas, nuts, etc.
- **intensity** *(exercise)* --- the more intensity, the less rest time between sets
- **load** *(weight)* --- something that is being carried
- **frame** *(body)* --- the size and shape of a person or animal's body
- **gain** *(increase)* --- an increase or improvement in something
- **bench press** --- an exercise where you lie down and push a weight up
- **break** *(record)* --- to do sth. better than the best record we know
- **push** *(work hard)* --- to make someone work hard
- **squat** *(exercise)* --- an exercise where you sit in the air and stand up
- **deadlift** --- an exercise where you pick a weight up from the floor
- **put sb./sth. to the test** --- to find out how good sb. or sth. is.
- **powerlifting** --- the sport of the bench press, squat, and deadlift
- **go all out** --- to use all of your energy to do something
- **lead up to** --- to happen until something bigger happens
- **sadistic** --- getting pleasure from hurting people
- **endure** *(suffer)* --- to suffer something difficult without giving up

Big Fish

- **meet** *[noun]* --- a sports event where people compete
- **class** *(competition)* --- one of the different groups in a competition
- **squeak** *(succeed)* --- to succeed only by a small amount
- **victory** --- winning a game, competition, war, election, etc.
- **put up** *(try)* --- to make a great effort in trying to achieve sth.
- **respectable** *(good)* --- pretty good
- **move** *(action)* --- an action you take to try to achieve something
- **seek** *(try)* --- to try to find, get, or do something
- **aspiration** *(wish)* --- something you wish to achieve
- **potentially** --- possibly in the future
- **for that matter** --- used to show something else is also true
- **terrify** --- to make someone extremely afraid
- **hunger** *(desire)* --- a strong feeling of really wanting something
- **driving force** --- the reason why something does something
- **dark** (**sad**) --- sad and without any hope
- **take hold** --- to grow strong or have complete control over sb./sth.
- **self-destructive** --- doing things to hurt yourself
- **crave** --- to have a strong feeling of really wanting something
- **altogether** *(completely)* --- completely
- **process** *(emotion)* --- to think about sth. so that you can accept it
- **emptiness** *(feeling)* --- a sad feeling of having no purpose or interest

- **destined** *(future)* --- certain to happen or do sth. in the future
- **all-star** *[adjective]* --- having many famous or talented people
- **world-class** --- one of the best in the world
- **for once** --- this time *(which is not usual)*
- **content** *[adjective]* --- happy and satisfied with a situation
- **realization** *(awareness)* --- the moment you really understand sth.
- **being** *(creature)* --- a living thing
- **infinite** --- without limits or extremely large
- **potential** --- the possibility to develop or achieve something
- **subside (calm)** --- to become weaker or less extreme
- **quest** --- a long and difficult search for something
- **fulfillment** *(feeling)* --- a feeling of being satisfied with your life
- **modest** *(not big)* --- not large or expensive
- **tap into** --- to use or connect someone to a resource
- **in the first place** --- originally

Comprehension Questions

1. If someone is a competitive spirit at their core, it means...
    A) they like hunting.
    B) they compete against spirits.
    C) they are competing at a world-class level.
    D) they love to compete and win.

2. How did Rhonda treat her classmates?
    A) She turned them into minnows for her to eat.
    B) She bullied them during tests.
    C) She was kind and friendly to them directly.
    D) She was respectful and even fed them.

3. How well did Rhonda do in university?
    A) She graduated at the top of her class.
    B) She did well but couldn't compete with the smartest there.
    C) She became a lawyer and a doctor.
    D) All of the above

4. If a workout is intense, it means that...
    A) it's very difficult.
    B) the rest periods during the workout are short.
    C) you will grow stronger by the end.
    D) All of the above

5. Which of the following exercises uses mostly the upper body?
    A) Bench Press
    B) Squat
    C) Deadlift
    D) Powerlifting

6. How did Rhonda train for the powerlifting meet?
    A) She endured sad workouts leading up to the event.
    B) She went all out and trained extremely hard.
    C) She was addicted to progress.
    D) She barely squeaked by with a victory.

7. What were Rhonda's aspirations after winning the competition?
    A) To compete in the Olympics and start a business
    B) She had no aspirations after winning.
    C) To become an alcoholic
    D) To open her own gym or start a line of supplements

8. Why was Rhonda depressed?
    A) A dark and self-destructive force took over the world.
    B) She was content with her death.
    C) She didn't drink enough.
    D) She had strong feelings of emptiness and despair.

9. According to the story, which of the following is infinite?
    A) Human beings' ability to care
    B) The amount of potential
    C) Human beings' ability to imagine and achieve things
    D) The amount of realizations

10. Why was Rhonda so competitive in the first place?
    A) She was on a quest to find fulfillment in a modest lifestyle.
    B) She was destined to be an all-star student and athlete.
    C) She was able to tap into her energy to be competitive.
    D) The story does not say.

CHAPTER SIX:

MAGIC AND MIGHT

A **goblin cried out** in fear. But it **was no use**. With a quick **swing** of a long **sword**, its head was immediately removed from its body.

The owner of the sword was Dreylor, who was on the hunt for great **treasures**. Dreylor was not the greatest at **combat**, but he did have many valuable skills. **For one**, he had **a keen eye**. He could see hidden enemies and objects better than almost anyone else. With Dreylor at your side, you're never surprised by **ambushes** or dangerous **traps**. For this reason, he had been chosen to accompany two other treasure hunters through the goblin **lair**.

"Just a little farther up ahead, and we'll reach it," spoke Jorgen. He raised his **battle ax** to check it. **Dripping** from the ax's blade was goblin blood. And that he could not accept. He considered himself a strong **warrior** but *not* a **barbarian**. Only a barbarian would allow blood to **stain** his own nice clothes. He took out a cloth to clean his **blade** before continuing on.

The group continued down the cave and reached a **ravine** that was over ten meters wide. The bridge to cross the ravine had been cut from the other side. It was now **dangling beneath** their feet. Doom **awaited** anyone unlucky enough to fall in. Looking up, the group could see a **blinding** light through a **crack** in the ceiling of the cave. The three had not seen any daylight since starting their mission early in the morning.

Dreylor and Jorgen started coming up with ideas on how to cross the **massive** gap. But then, the third member of the **party** stepped forward.

A long, **tattered cloak** covered the face and body, but the hands could be seen moving in circles. **Mysterious runes** covered the hands with all sorts of ancient writing. Words in an unknown language came from the cloaked traveler. The runes began to **glow** bright blue. The **chant** was not more than a few seconds long, and at the end, the circling, glowing hands quickly **shot up**.

Moments later, bright **particles** of light seemed to appear in the air. They began **drawing** closer together over the ravine. And then, they started forming into a large **structure**. Now the shape of an **arch** could be seen. It was a bridge, one with beautiful **prismatic** colors. It was also **semi-transparent**. But when the cloaked **figure** stepped upon it, the other two knew it was safe to cross.

Turning towards the two other **companions**, a face of a young woman could be seen through the **hood**. Alyssa was her name. "The **spell** won't last for more than a minute. Off we go now," she spoke with a **eloquent** voice.

The three walked quickly across and had safely managed to reach the other side. They were surely coming to the end of the **cavern**. But what exactly **lay in store** for them? Would it be the stolen **stash** of goods as **rumored**? If so, what would be **guarding** it?

Up ahead, the party approached a **crude staircase** made of stone. After climbing it, they finally found the answers to their burning questions. A large room opened up before them, and all was revealed.

There in the far-left corner was the stash of stolen **merchant** goods. Returning them would result in a great reward. Selling them and **pocketing** the money would make anyone as rich as a merchant.

But there were also **orcs**, three to be exact. And they were not in the mood to share their **ill-gotten** gains. **Vicious grunts** filled the room moments after the party entered. Now there was only one way to **resolve** this situation.

Jorgen **rushed in** with his battle-ax, wasting no time talking. The orcs **blocked** his attack with their **scimitars**. They then took turns **striking back**. Alyssa **took aim** with her **staff** and fired ice magic at the green creatures. Dreylor, however, was nowhere to be seen.

Facing three scimitars from three **savage** orcs would scare away most fighters. Even Jorgen showed signs of fear in his eyes as he heard the **whooshing** sounds of blades barely missing his ears. He could no longer attack as he was busy blocking, **dodging**, and trying not to be **cleaved in two**. A lucky swing from below managed to get through and made a **gash** down his leg. A cry of pain followed. And the orcs **grinned** in response.

The green **brutes** approached to finish the job when a **spear** of ice flew between the shoulders of two of them. It barely missed due to Alyssa's unfortunate aiming. But it was enough to **stop them in their tracks**. Now the monsters were **torn between** which **adventurer** to attack.

When the orcs turned their heads to communicate, there was a shock. They discovered that they **were down to** just two. One was lying on the floor in a pool of its own blood, **fatally wounded**. It appeared that whoever killed their orc **comrade** had disappeared back into the shadows. It might have even been a ghost **for all they knew**.

While the two remaining orcs stood around confused, Jorgen took the opportunity to strike back. He was able to **catch one off guard** and **slash** its arm holding the scimitar. The extreme pain **sent** the orc into a **rage**. The orc **gripped** his weapon even harder and swung **wildly** at the warrior in every direction.

The rage had made him extremely dangerous, but after each swing, he was also extremely **vulnerable**. With a **well-timed** ice spear from Alyssa, he was frozen solid in a block of ice.

The final orc gave a look of defeat when he knew he could no longer win. He ran deeper into the cave away from the path the adventurers had come from. Just before he was out of sight, a knife thrown from a dark corner landed right in the back of his head, bringing the fight to an end.

Dreylor stepped out from the shadows, putting his long sword back into its **sheath**. "You make a great **meat shield**, Jorgen! I call first **dibs** on the **loot**, though. I did get most of the kills."

"Oh **come on**! This was a team effort, and you know it! You can't just go around getting the best loot because you got a few lucky kills," said Jorgen.

"Sure I can. My character runs towards the gold and picks up as much as he can carry," said Dreylor.

"That's a **load of crap**, and you know it," said Alyssa, although now with the voice of a man. "If you keep playing like this, don't even bother coming back next week."

"Alright. Fine," replied the player playing Dreylor. He picked up his **dice**. "I'll **roll** a **sleight of hand**," he said with a calm voice while throwing the dice. "I got 15. Now roll for a **spot** skill check."

"**You know what?**" the player playing Jorgen said with anger while standing up. "I'm done. I'm taking my dice and going home," he shouted.

And **with that**, the game had come to an end.

Magic and Might

Vocabulary and Grammar

- **might** *[noun]* --- great strength or power
- **goblin** --- a small, ugly creature in stories that causes trouble
- **cry out** --- to make a loud sound because you are hurt or afraid
- **be no use** --- to be useless
- **swing** *(hit)* --- a quick movement to try to hit someone or sth.
- **sword** --- a long, sharp metal weapon used in the past
- **treasure** *(things)* --- very valuable things like gold and silver
- **combat** --- a fight or fighting
- **for one (thing)** --- used to give one reason when there are many
- **a keen eye (for something)** --- an ability to notice something
- **ambush** --- a surprise attack by sb. who was hiding and waiting
- **trap** *(equipment)* --- equipment for catching or hurting sb. or sth.
- **lair** --- a place where a wild animal or a dangerous person lives
- **battle ax** --- a heavy metal weapon used in the past mostly for cutting
- **dripping** --- very wet
- **warrior** --- a person who fights or has fought in a battle or war
- **barbarian** --- sb. people consider as dirty and violent
- **stain** *(mark)* --- to leave a spot on sth. that is hard to remove
- **blade** *(sharp)* --- the flat, sharp part of a tool or weapon that cuts
- **ravine** --- a very deep and narrow valley with steep sides

- **dangle** *(move)* --- to move while hanging
- **beneath** *(under)* --- under or below
- **await** *(will happen)* --- to be going to happen to someone
- **blinding** --- so bright that you cannot see
- **crack** *(space)* --- a very narrow space where sth. is breaking apart
- **massive** --- very large
- **party** *(small group)* --- a group of people who are doing sth. together
- **tattered** --- old, torn, and damaged
- **cloak** --- a long coat without sleeves that hangs at the shoulders
- **mysterious** --- strange or not understood
- **rune** *(magic)* --- marks or letters used in magic in stories
- **glow** *(light)* --- to produce a small light for a period of time
- **chant** *(repeat)* --- to repeat or sing a few words or phrases many times
- **shoot** *(move)* --- to move in a direction very suddenly and quickly
- **particle** *(piece)* --- an extremely small piece of something
- **draw** *(move)* --- to move in a particular direction
- **structure** *(building)* --- sth. large that is built from many parts
- **arch** *(shape)* --- something that has a round shape at the top
- **prismatic** *(color)* --- having many very bright colors
- **semi-transparent** --- able to be seen through to some level
- **figure** *(shape)* --- the shape of a person you can't see clearly

Magic and Might

- **companion** *(friend)* --- sb. you travel or spend a lot of time with
- **hood** *(coat)* --- the part of some clothes that covers your head
- **spell** *(magic)* --- words or actions that have magic power in a story
- **eloquent** --- good at speaking and able to persuade people
- **cavern** --- a large cave
- **lie in store** --- to be going to happen in the future
- **stash** *[noun]* --- an amount of sth. that has been kept hidden
- **rumor** *[verb]* --- to be reported but may or may not be true
- **guard** *(protect)* --- to protect sb. or sth. from being attacked or stolen
- **crude** *(simple)* --- simply made but without skill
- **staircase** --- a set of stairs
- **merchant** --- a person or business that buys and sells goods
- **pocket** *(keep)* --- to get and keep money that doesn't belong to you
- **orc** --- a bad and ugly creature in stories that likes fighting
- **ill-gotten** --- got in a way that is not legal or fair
- **vicious** *(violent)* --- very violent or cruel
- **grunt** *(sound)* --- a short, low sound made by a person or animal
- **resolve** *(solve)* --- to find a solution to a problem
- **rush** *(go quickly)* --- to (make somebody) go or do sth. quickly
- **block** *(hit)* --- to stop a hit, ball, or object by using something
- **scimitar** --- a short sword that bends near the top

- **strike back** --- to attack someone who has attacked you
- **take aim** --- to point a weapon before you shoot or throw it
- **staff** *(stick)* --- a long stick used to fight or to make walking easier
- **savage** *(violent)* --- very violent or cruel
- **whooshing** --- moving very quickly making the sound of wind
- **dodge** *(move)* --- to move quickly to avoid being hit by sth.
- **cleave** --- to cut something into two pieces in a violent way
- **in two** --- in(to) two pieces
- **gash** *[noun]* --- a long deep cut *(usually in your skin)*
- **grin** *[verb]* --- to smile with a wide smile
- **brute** *(animal)* --- a large strong animal
- **spear** *(weapon)* --- a long weapon with a sharp end
- **stop sb. in their tracks** --- to make sb. stop moving or doing sth.
- **torn between** --- unable to decide between two choices
- **adventurer** --- someone who likes going on adventures
- **be down to** *(amount)* --- to be or have a smaller amount than before
- **fatally** *(death)* --- in a way that will kill
- **wounded** *(injured)* --- injured
- **comrade** *(friend)* --- a friend *(usually one you fight together with)*
- **for all sb. knows** --- used when sb. doesn't know something
- **catch somebody off guard** --- to surprise somebody

- **slash** *(cut)* --- to cut someone or something in a violent way
- **send** *(cause)* --- to cause sb. or sth. to react in a particular way
- **rage** *(feeling)* --- a feeling of being extremely angry
- **grip** *(hold)* --- to hold in a way that is very tight
- **wildly** *(not controlled)* --- in a way that is not controlled
- **vulnerable** --- weak and easily hurt physically or mentally
- **well-timed** --- happening at the right time
- **sheath** *(weapon)* --- a cover for a sword or knife
- **meat shield** --- *(informal)* sb. used to take hits so you don't get hit
- **dibs** --- *(informal)* the right to have something
- **loot** *(battle)* --- money or goods taken from a defeated enemy
- **come on** *(disagree)* --- *(informal)* used to disagree with sb. or sth.
- **load of crap** --- *(informal)* something that is very bad or not true
- **dice** --- an object with (six) sides with numbers used in games
- **roll** *(dice)* --- to throw dice in a game
- **sleight of hand** *(hands)* --- speed and skill of hands used in tricks
- **spot** *(notice)* --- to notice someone or something
- **You know what?** --- *(informal)* used to introduce sth. surprising
- **with that** --- and then

Comprehension Questions

1. In the party, who could see hidden enemies and traps the best?
    A) Dreylor
    B) Jorgen
    C) Alyssa
    D) The orcs

2. If you fell into a very large ravine, what would likely happen?
    A) You would turn into a bird and fly away.
    B) You would fall to your death.
    C) You would find treasure.
    D) You would land on giant pillows.

3. How did the party cross the ravine?
    A) They crossed a bridge that was dangling below.
    B) Alyssa cast a spell that formed a bridge to cross.
    C) Dreylor and Jorgen came up with an idea to cross the gap.
    D) They drew closer together to form an arch structure.

4. What was the rumor that was mentioned in the story?
    A) There was a stash of stolen merchant goods in a cavern.
    B) There were goblins and orcs guarding a cavern.
    C) There was a crude staircase made of stone in the cavern.
    D) All of the above

5. What did the adventurers find at the end of the cavern?
    A) Three players arguing over loot
    B) A stash of stolen goods and gold and three orcs
    C) A knife in the back of an orc's head
    D) Dice rolling and skill checks

Magic and Might

6. How was Jorgen injured during the fight?
    A) His leg was cut deeply.
    B) His arm was crushed by a hammer.
    C) His body was stabbed.
    D) His head was chopped off.

7. What kind of magic did Alyssa fight with?
    A) She cast spells using magic runes written on her hands.
    B) She took aim with her staff and threw it like a spear.
    C) She cast spears made of ice to freeze enemies.
    D) None of the above

8. How did the first orc die?
    A) It disappeared.
    B) It was killed by a ghost.
    C) It drowned in a pool of its own blood.
    D) It was killed by Dreylor.

9. How did the last orc die?
    A) It didn't. It got away.
    B) It was killed by a ghost.
    C) It was killed by a knife landing in the back of its head.
    D) It was killed by Alyssa.

10. What was Dreylor trying to do with his sleight of hand?
    A) He was trying to perform a magic trick.
    B) He was trying to steal the players' dice.
    C) He was trying to steal the treasure.
    D) He was trying to steal from his teammates' wallets.

CHAPTER SEVEN:

MIND GAMES

When most people play games, it's as a **casual** hobby. They play to relax and seek entertainment after a long day or week of school or work. These sessions typically last from just a few minutes to several hours. They play many different games. And at the end of the day, they are just games.

Calvin was not your typical **gamer**, however. To him, the future was gaming. There was a growing competitive scene for video games, and the prize **pools** were getting larger every year. He grew up hearing stories of teenagers and young adults **walking away with** thousands of dollars from tournaments.

Why such huge prizes for beating someone in a video game? Any kind of game can become competitive, but not every game is fun to watch. When played at the **pro** level, certain games become amazing **spectator sports** just like soccer or football. They attract millions of people across the world. Millions of people watching means companies will pay millions of dollars to advertise to them. **Thus**, a billion-dollar industry was born.

The cash prizes, the **glory**, and the adventure were all too **tempting** to Calvin. To make it big was his dream.

Mind Games

But there was a **catch**. You had to be the best. And the competition was filled with **hardcore** players whose whole lives **revolved around** not just gaming but usually one game.

Calvin just had to find his one game. Calvin neither had the quick **reflexes** required for shooting or fighting games, nor did he have the right team for team-based games.

But he was naturally drawn towards strategy games. He found them easy to learn how to play. And he was obsessed with learning new techniques and strategies from players **ranked** higher than himself. Hours would fly by as he tested new ideas against online **opponents**. Each victory was **proof** that his time in and out of the game was paying off. It was highly **rewarding**. And it brought him a **thrill** he did not get anywhere else.

At school, he was brilliant but lazy. Learning from teachers and books came **somewhat** easy, but it didn't excite him all too much. Storing large amounts of information in his head was kind of like a game, although a boring one. It helped a little to think of homework as practice games where he **honed** his abilities. Tests were then the high-level games that determined your true skill. All of this worked well enough to make him a **B student**.

Calvin's friends at his high school were also gamers. At lunchtime and between classes, they would get excited discussing the latest and **upcoming** games. The group argued about what made games great and other games not so great. Conversations between them were full of **mutual** feelings of passion and love for video games.

Each week, the group picked one specific game to play together on Saturday. They would **take turns** meeting at each other's houses. There they spent all day and night **bonding** together while enjoying their **pastime**.

One week, Calvin and his friends decided to play a strategy game called *Techcraft*. The goal of the game was simple. Players **duel** other players by **crafting** weapons using the resources they find and fight over across the game field.

The more resources you **acquire**, the higher **tech** and more effective weapons you can make. Players start with **primitive** tools and weapons but can **upgrade** them. With enough resources, they can start crafting **medieval** tools and weapons and eventually modern ones. The strategy of the game is found in gathering more resources than your opponent and in **picking fights** you can win over **contested** areas on the map. Collect enough resources, and you will **overpower** your enemy and win the game.

For that week and even the following week, the group was absolutely mesmerized by the game. They **couldn't put it down**. Matches would become very competitive, and the room would **gradually** get more **tense** by the minute. Whether you were playing or just **spectating**, the game could **hold** every last bit of your attention until everything was all over.

After a few weeks of play, however, Calvin had learned several tips and **tricks** by watching more advanced players online. Soon enough, he was **crushing** his friends in embarrassing **landslide** victories. In fact, he became so good at the game that he never lost a single game to his friends ever again. As a result, everybody but Calvin started to lose interest in the game. He offered to teach them pro-level strategies, but it was too late. They had moved on.

The group continued to **rotate** game after game, but Calvin's passion for *Techcraft* only kept growing. It was the only game he wanted to play. He played for hours each day, honing his skills against players at his level and higher. He went to bed every night thinking about the game, even dreaming about one day competing with the top-level players. There was something about **grinding** his way to the top that excited him deeply.

Afternoons home from school were dedicated to practicing new strategies. Weekends were for **reading up on** new tips and tricks and to watch tournaments streamed live. And of course, nights were long due to **extended** play sessions with new friends he met through the online community.

His obsession slowly started to **take a toll** on his life in the real world.

In school, he tried to get a passing grade by doing the least amount of work, but this strategy quickly **fell apart**. His homework assignments were **turned in** late or even **incomplete**. He began to fall asleep in class due to lack of sleep. And as a result, his test scores started to drop.

Calvin was also **losing touch with** his friends. Every last free moment he had went into one game, so there was no time to hang out after school or on weekends. His friends thought he was **taking** the game much too **seriously**, and they stopped inviting him to their **meetups**. The **isolation**, however, let him know who his real friends were.

Calvin started to gain fame and **status** online as a highly **skilled** player. Here he had a community of people to bond over a game that not even the **nerdy** gamers at his school cared enough about. The internet had both isolated him from real life friends and given him new friends that shared a very **niche** hobby they all loved.

He talked with thousands of players across the world in **chat rooms** and **forums**. They watched his games and **clips** from them across social media, and many were **impressed** by what they saw.

Calvin's mind was an **encyclopedia** on how to master the game. He could remember and **apply** almost everything he learned watching and reading. By mixing and matching strategies used by different professional players, he was able to create his own unique and effective play style.

His victories in online tournaments were enough to earn him a spot at an **invitational** event. It was the opportunity of a **lifetime**.

The best players of the game gathered online for a chance at the **grand** prize of $50,000. Only one person would walk away with the prize money, and it was going to be the top player of all the top players.

There were several from the community **cheering** Calvin **on**, but the voices cheering for the most famous players were nearly 100 times louder. Suddenly, it seemed like most of his supporters had **abandoned** him. This shook his **confidence** significantly. But the idea that he was going in as the **underdog** helped calm him down.

Despite being a **nervous wreck**, Calvin did surprisingly well the first round. He was able to put his full attention and focus on continuously **spying on** his opponent and preparing his ambush. His opponent **suffered** big **losses** after a surprise attack by Calvin. As a result, his opponent played extremely **conservatively** while being afraid to **take** any **risks**. This allowed Calvin to control the playing field easily, gather more resources, and build a much stronger character to win the game in the end.

With his first major tournament match victory, his confidence was at an **all-time high**. Now more messages of support from his fans started to appear on social media. His **momentum** was building.

The next **rounds** were **by no means** easy, however. They were much closer than the first match. But as the games **progressed**, he learned that he could handle the pressure better than most players. In fact, he **thrived on** it. The more pressure the better, he thought.

Mind Games

All players make mistakes and are affected by them, but Calvin's mistakes didn't upset him all that much.

Before he knew it, Calvin had arrived at the **semi-final** round! Even he was amazed he had made it this far in his first major tournament. All his hard work had paid off.

The next match, however, would be a true test of his abilities. It would be against Johnathan, the player ranked #1 in the world. So much **adrenaline** was running through his head that he could not process the situation whatsoever.

So instead, he pulled out his smartphone to check the messages he received. He could barely focus but managed to read the first 50 or so. There was **overwhelming** support for him from an **unimaginable** number of people. But there was one message that immediately stood out from the rest. It read, "Try not to kill yourself after you get humiliated today. Good luck!"

Those 12 words sent Calvin into a rage. All he could think about was typing out the **nastiest** reply he could come up with. He stood up and **paced** around the room while thinking of the perfect **comeback**. Ten minutes had gone by. Then 20 had passed. But before he could type out his insult, it was time for the semi-final match. He wanted to **slam** his keyboard on something, but he needed it to play.

The match had begun. Calvin needed to **put pressure on** Johnathan to gain an advantage. He spied on his every move, waiting for his opportunity to strike. When he did, it would be game over from that point. He just needed to be patient. "Wait for it," he kept telling himself. Be ready. It's coming.

But Johnathan simply did not make any mistakes of any kind. It was Calvin who was making all the mistakes. Every move Calvin made was expected and **countered** by the champion. He had never played against someone who played so **flawlessly** and beautifully.

There was no advantage he could secure. And it was all over after just 15 minutes.

The match was a complete **blowout**. After the game, Calvin put his hands on his head in disbelief. **How on earth** could he ever compete with *that*? There was no way. How was it even possible to play that fast? He had watched videos of Johnathan's games, but to play against him was an absolute nightmare.

That night, Calvin lay in his bed, **reflecting** on the journey that led him to this point. He reached for his smartphone to read others' opinions about the game but then remembered the awful message he came across earlier. There were hundreds of encouraging messages he had received, most of which were nice and wonderful to read. But that one message had **ruined** them all. What good was reading posts from fans if one bad one could **infuriate** him?

Who would send such a message? Was it from one of Johnathan's fans? Why did he care so much about it? How could reading a post from a stranger upset him so much? He was suffering from depression, but aren't most people suffering as well, he thought.

Sadness filled his heart. Tears started forming at the corner of his eyes. And now he felt more alone than ever before. **Streams** of tears flowed from his eyes as he wished he was gone from this world.

Calvin awoke the next morning and went for a long walk around his neighborhood. He thought about where to go from here with his life.

He had invested more than a thousand hours into this game and had made it to the semi-finals of a major tournament. He was proud of his achievement without a doubt.

What had it cost him, though? His grades dropped to D's in most of his classes, and he was even failing a few classes. He had made no time for his friends, so they stopped inviting him to hang out together. And his **belly** had gained at least 15 pounds due to a lack of exercise and him living off of junk food.

What would it cost to beat Johnathan? It would not take a thousand hours but multiple thousands of hours of practice to win. He would have to sacrifice everything to even have a chance at defeating a champion. For the first time in a long time, Calvin felt how easily he could ruin his life with such a decision.

He saw his life as one large strategy game. Strategy, at its core, comes down to **risk assessment**, he figured. All moves in a game involve risk. Winning was done not by taking big risks for big rewards. It was done by taking the smallest risks for the largest rewards.

And so it was time for a break. It was time to **reconnect** with old friends and his schoolwork. It was time to bring balance back into his life.

Life was waiting for him. Life always waits to welcome us back.

Vocabulary and Grammar

- **mind games** *(people)* --- a game to try to act smarter than sb. else

- **mind game** *(puzzle)* --- a game to exercise your mind

- **casual** *(hobby)* --- doing a hobby sometimes but not a lot

- **gamer** --- a person who likes playing video games

- **pool** *(money)* --- money given to players who do well in a game

- **walk away with something** --- to win something easily

- **pro** [*adjective*] --- professional

- **spectator sport** --- a sport that many people enjoy watching

- **thus** --- in this way or as a result
- **glory (respect)** --- great respect from people you get from your success
- **tempting** --- making you want to do or have it
- **catch (problem)** --- a hidden problem in sth. that seems good
- **hardcore (determined)** --- giving all your time and energy to sth.
- **revolve around sth.** --- to have sth. as the most important part
- **reflex (ability)** --- the ability to react quickly without thinking
- **rank (have)** --- to have a level of importance compared to others
- **opponent (competition)** --- a person you compete against
- **proof (information)** --- information that shows something is true
- **rewarding** --- makes you feel satisfied
- **thrill** --- a strong feeling of excitement
- **somewhat** --- to some amount or level
- **hone (develop)** --- to develop and improve something
- **B student** --- a student that is good but not excellent
- **upcoming** --- happening soon
- **mutual** --- shared by two or more people
- **take turns** --- to do something with others but one at a time
- **bond (create)** --- to (make sb.) create a close connection with sb. (else)
- **pastime** --- hobby
- **duel (fight)** --- to fight sb. with swords or guns in a formal match

Mind Games

- **craft** *[verb]* --- to make something using skill
- **acquire** *(get)* --- to get something
- **tech** *(technology)* --- technology
- **primitive** *(history)* --- relating to a very early stage of human history
- **upgrade** *(start)* --- to start using a better version of something
- **medieval** --- a time in history around 476-1453 AD
- **pick a fight** --- to start a fight with someone
- **contested** *(disputed)* --- being fought over
- **overpower** *(defeat)* --- to defeat someone by using greater power
- **not put sth. down** --- to be unable to stop doing sth. until the end
- **gradually** --- slowly over time or a distance
- **tense** *(situation)* --- making you feel nervous and not relaxed
- **spectate** --- to watch an event *(usually a sports event)*
- **hold** *(attention)* --- to keep someone's attention or interest
- **trick** *(method)* --- a quick and effective method
- **crush** *(defeat)* --- to defeat someone completely
- **landslide** *(victory)* --- a win where sb. is completely defeated
- **rotate** *(take turns)* --- to (make something) happen in turns
- **grind** *(work)* --- to work hard
- **read up on** --- to read a lot about something
- **extended** --- long or longer than normal

- **take a toll on** --- to damage someone or something over time
- **fall apart** *(fail)* --- to fail or stop working well
- **turn sth. in** *(give)* --- to give sth. to someone in authority
- **incomplete** --- not complete
- **lose touch with sb.** --- to stop communicating with sb.
- **take sth./sb. seriously** --- to think that sth./sb. is serious
- **meetup** --- an informal meeting
- **isolation** --- being separated and not connected to others
- **status** *(high)* --- high respect and importance given by other people
- **skilled** *(person)* --- having the abilities to do something well
- **nerdy** --- extremely interested in one subject and not very social
- **niche** *[adjective]* --- interesting to only a small number of people
- **chat room** --- an area on the internet where people exchange messages
- **forum** *(internet)* --- a website where people can discuss topics
- **clip** *(video)* --- a short part from a video, film, or TV program
- **impressed** *[adjective]* --- feeling respect for someone or sth.
- **encyclopedia** --- a collection of knowledge about one or many topics
- **apply** *(use)* --- to use something for a practical purpose
- **invitational** --- a sports event where competitors have to be invited
- **lifetime** --- the period of time someone is alive or something lasts
- **grand** *(largest)* --- the largest and most important

Mind Games

- **cheer (sb. on)** --- to shout or to encourage sb. in a competition
- **abandon** *(person)* --- to leave someone when you should stay
- **confidence** *(you)* --- the belief that you can do something well
- **underdog** --- a person or group that is not likely to win or succeed
- **nervous wreck** --- someone who is very nervous and worried
- **spy on** --- to watch someone or something in a secret way
- **suffer something** --- to experience something unpleasant
- **loss** *(disadvantage)* --- a disadvantage caused by sth. being taken away
- **conservatively** *(carefully)* --- carefully and in a way to avoid risk
- **take a risk** --- to do something that might have a bad result
- **all-time high** --- the highest something has ever been
- **momentum** --- power gained by movement or a series of events
- **round** *(competition)* --- a game or a series of games in a competition
- **by no means** --- not at all
- **progress** *(develop)* --- to develop or improve
- **thrive on** --- to enjoy or succeed at sth. most people would not
- **before somebody knows it** --- surprisingly and quickly
- **semi-final** --- one of the two games in a competition before the final
- **adrenaline** --- this gives your body energy when you're excited or scared
- **overwhelming** --- very strong or very great
- **unimaginable** --- very difficult to imagine

- **nasty** *(mean)* --- very mean
- **pace** --- to walk up and down many times when you're angry or worried
- **comeback** *(reply)* --- a clever reply to sth. bad said about you
- **slam** *(put)* --- to put or hit sth. against a surface with a lot of force
- **put pressure on sb.** --- to try to force or persuade sb. to do sth.
- **counter** *(prevent)* --- to do sth. to stop sth. from happening
- **flawlessly** --- perfectly
- **blowout** *(game)* --- an easy win
- **how/why/etc. on earth** --- used when you're surprised or angry
- **reflect** *(think)* --- to think carefully about something
- **ruin** *(damage)* --- to damage sth. so badly it loses all its value
- **infuriate** --- to make someone extremely angry
- **stream** *(flow)* --- a continuous flow of things or people
- **belly** *(body)* --- stomach
- **risk assessment** --- the examination of risks involved in an action
- **reconnect** --- to connect again after being separated

Mind Games

Comprehension Questions

1. What makes a game a spectator sport?
    A) The many people watching it
    B) The many companies sponsoring events
    C) The many players competing in it
    D) The many prizes being awarded

2. Why was Calvin drawn towards strategy games?
    A) He didn't have the reflexes needed for combat.
    B) He didn't have the right team to compete with.
    C) He was thrilled to have proof of his rewards.
    D) He loved learning and testing new strategies against people.

3. What did Calvin's group of friends do every Saturday?
    A) They took turns bonding with each other.
    B) They got together to play games.
    C) They bonded with their pastime.
    D) They picked one specific game and took turns playing it.

4. What is a landslide victory?
    A) A victory after a very close game
    B) A victory at the grand finals of a tournament
    C) A victory where one side completely destroys the other
    D) A victory from one side that was completely unexpected

5. Why did Calvin's grades start to drop?
    A) He spent his afternoons playing educational games.
    B) He stayed up all night cramming for tests.
    C) He tried to do the least amount of work possible.
    D) None of the above

6. How did Calvin create his own play style?
    A) He had a natural intuition on how to play the game.
    B) He was a super smart and gifted person.
    C) He improvised everything.
    D) He mixed and matched strategies from top-level players.

7. Why did Calvin feel abandoned in the story?
    A) His parents didn't spend much time with him.
    B) His confidence was shaken significantly.
    C) Many of his supporters were cheering for other players.
    D) His friends stopped inviting him to hang out.

8. How did Calvin handle pressure during top-level games?
    A) He made mistakes like all players.
    B) His mistakes upset him very much.
    C) He actually enjoyed it.
    D) He performed just as well as any other player.

9. If you slam a computer keyboard on something, ...
    A) It will restart the computer.
    B) It will delete all the files on the computer.
    C) It will knock the dirt out of it.
    D) It will break.

10. Which of the following is the best strategy for winning?
    A) High-risk moves with potentially high rewards
    B) High-risk moves with potentially low rewards
    C) Low-risk moves with potentially high rewards
    D) Low-risk moves with potentially low rewards

CHAPTER EIGHT:

MODERATION AND EXTREMISM

S arah was young, beautiful, and single, but that did little to **alleviate** her problems. Having been raised by parents with deep issues of unhappiness, her childhood was full of intense emotional pain.

Her mother was quite **abusive** and had her own history of **mistreatment** from her parents. She was on permanent **disability** due to a back injury she suffered many years ago. Having never to work again **left** her with nothing but leisure **time on her hands.** She spent her days watching TV, **binge drinking**, and starting arguments with Sarah and her little brothers at every opportunity. Sarah quickly learned to avoid **confrontations** with her mother at all costs, especially when she was drinking.

Her father did the best he could to provide for the family. He had a stable job, was able to afford a safe place for everyone to live, and put food on the table. But he would always come home at night exhausted and stressed out, and Sarah's mom regularly **took advantage of** this. She picked fights with him about the most **trivial** things and insulted him to no end. Eventually, he would **snap**, and intense **shouting matches** would occur, sometimes turning violent.

One morning shortly after Sarah **turned** 11, her father left to get his morning coffee. But he never came back. Just like that he was gone **for good**.

And now there was nothing between Sarah and her brothers and their mother. If she avoided her mother, it meant the younger ones would become her targets. She would not let that happen.

Because of her **troubled** home life, Sarah **struggled** frequently at school. She had learned to avoid confrontation as a child, so she never bothered to raise her hand to ask or answer questions. If she never tried, she would never fail, she figured. Being **temporarily** free from her mother was good enough anyway.

And she had plenty of friends, who were much nicer to her. They helped her with her schoolwork and encouraged her during class. Outside of class, her **circle** of friends was always cracking jokes, making it easier to laugh even on the toughest of days. Some of the girls were even ambitious and would talk about wanting to go to college to become doctors and lawyers. Life in general seemed much brighter and hopeful being around them.

Sarah's mom, however, became **increasingly** harder and harder to deal with. Alcohol had become a bit boring for her, so she **turned to opioids** to cope with reality. Fortunately, she was very **passive** after each **dose** and didn't cause any trouble around the house. But when she ran out of her **prescription**, the **withdrawal** symptoms made her both angry and violent. Sarah took the full force of the damage, as she couldn't **bear** the thought of her brothers suffering instead.

While she protected her brothers from danger, they saw and heard much of what happened. Their mother had a few **close calls** after **overdosing** on opioids. Sarah was told by her mom to not call **911** because if she did the police would take her and her brothers away from their home forever.

Moderation and Extremism

When she turned 18, she came to the decision to move out for good. If she was going to do anything with her life, she needed the space and freedom to start. Her brothers were now old enough to take care of themselves and their mother when necessary.

To pay the rent for her new apartment, she took a job as a **barista** at a local coffee shop. Sarah worked hard and gave the job everything she had. After all, she had nobody to **turn to** if she couldn't pay the bills. She was quickly promoted to a manager position after just a year.

There was one job at the shop she could not do, however. The store was located in a downtown area where many immigrants worked as **manual laborers**. These immigrants were **largely** from Spanish-speaking countries and spoke almost no English at all. They were able to order what they wanted but couldn't understand anything the staff spoke to them.

As a barista, it was Sarah's job to make each customer feel comfortable and at home. But she couldn't do that in English. And so the inspiration to learn Spanish **took root**.

In her free time, she used language learning apps and listened to audio lessons for several hours each week. Sarah was making fast progress and was amazed at how easy it was pick up simple phrases and vocabulary. Almost immediately, she started using what she learned with her customers at work. Her Spanish was **met with** surprised faces and joy.

Although when her customers spoke back to her in Spanish, she was now the one who couldn't understand. Many conversations repeated this same pattern, and after a while, it became clear. While she knew many phrases and words, she couldn't have a real conversation in Spanish.

She poured more and more time into learning as much Spanish as she could. She bought grammar books. She memorized vocabulary lists. She watched TV in Spanish while she was at home.

She even **got into** the habit of making flashcards on her smartphone and reviewing them for a few minutes every day.

Yet her rate of progress was slow and thus disappointing. Sarah would forget words. And there were hundreds of things she didn't know how to say to her customers. And she still had little idea of what customers were saying back to her. As a **C student**, she concluded she wasn't smart enough to become fluent.

One day, she was **catching up** with her friend Leah from school, whom she hadn't heard from in a long time. Leah was now a **sophomore** in college and planning to get her degree in chemistry. She mentioned that she was also taking French classes on the side, which immediately caught Sarah's attention. They had a similar hobby they could bond over. So Leah suggested they both go to a local **language exchange** event held at a coffee shop downtown.

The event took place on a Sunday afternoon. By the time Sarah and Leah arrived, there were nearly a hundred people sitting down and chatting with one another. The girls heard a variety of languages, including Spanish, French, German, Italian, and even Korean. After signing up at the door, they **split up** to join the language groups they were interested in.

Sarah found not just one but multiple native Spanish speakers to **converse** with. In each conversation, she **picked up** new words and wrote them down in the notebook she brought along. Communication was extremely slow, but she felt she was taking the necessary steps towards real progress.

One gentleman she spoke to was Gabriel. He was from Spain and had come to the language exchange to practice speaking English. After a few minutes of **small talk** and **chatter**, they learned they both had a similar past. He ran away from home at age 16 and took up various laboring jobs to support himself. From there he decided to travel around Europe, **migrating** to France and then

Germany in search of new experiences. While traveling and working across Europe, he taught himself both French and German.

After the event **officially** came to an end, Sarah found Leah and Gabriel chatting outside in French. She was **speechless** after hearing how beautifully and **fluently** he spoke. How could someone who had **dropped out** of high school learn so many different foreign languages? What was he doing differently than her?

She decided to approach him and ask him directly. Gabriel said that while moving to the target country certainly helped, it was not the **deciding** factor. He knew plenty of immigrant workers in France and Germany who could only speak their native language. According to him, what mattered most was what you did in your free time.

Gabriel spent the overwhelming majority of his time not studying but listening to and reading anything and everything he could in French, German, and English. **Occasionally**, he would go out with friends and socialize, but the vast majority of his time was spent immersing himself in different cultures. It was the only way he could understand all the different words and phrases native speakers used.

While on the train heading home, Sarah and Leah discussed what Gabriel had told them. They both agreed that his language skills were **nothing short of** impressive.

Leah didn't quite agree with Gabriel, however. As a college student working part-time, there was just no way she could dedicate that much time each day to learning. Besides, he learned all of those languages **out of necessity**, and she was learning French mostly as a hobby. Maybe she would reach fluency one day, but if it never happens, she would be OK with that. She **had nothing to prove**.

Sarah, on the other hand, reflected deeply on his words. She **desperately** wanted to speak fluently like Gabriel but for just one foreign language. The idea excited her more than anything else had in her life. There was a passion **burning** within her that she could not explain. Maybe it was her **ego**. Maybe it was because of her difficult past. If he could do it, so could she, she figured. She wasn't sure exactly where to start immersing, but she knew that the time to start was now.

Vocabulary and Grammar

- **moderation** *(idea)* --- the idea of not doing too much of sth.

- **extremism** --- ideas that are considered too extreme by most people

- **alleviate** --- to make something less painful or serious

- **abusive** *(words)* --- being cruel with words

- **mistreatment** --- treating someone in a cruel or unfair way

- **disability** *(money)* --- money paid to sb. who is too unhealthy to work

- **leave** *(remain)* --- to remain or make sth. happen as a result

- **time on somebody's hands** --- time when you are not busy

- **binge drinking** --- drinking lots of alcohol in a short time period

- **confrontation** --- an argument or a fight

- **take advantage of sth.** --- to use sth. available to you

- **trivial** --- not important or serious

- **snap** *(get angry)* --- to suddenly lose control of yourself and get angry

Moderation and Extremism

- **shouting match** --- an argument where people shout at each other
- **turn** *(age)* --- to become a particular age or time
- **for good** --- forever
- **troubled** *(difficult)* --- having a lot of problems
- **struggle** *(fail)* --- to be in danger of failing or losing
- **temporarily** --- in a way that lasts a short period of time
- **circle** *(of people)* --- a group of people who are connected by sth.
- **increasingly** --- more and more over time
- **turn to something** --- to start to do or use something bad
- **opioid** --- a strong drug that reduces pain that is hard to stop using
- **passive** *(behavior)* --- accepting what happens and not trying to change it
- **dose** *(medicine)* --- medicine taken at one time
- **prescription** *(medicine)* --- medicine ordered by a doctor or the order itself
- **withdrawal** *(drug)* --- the unpleasant effects when you stop using a drug
- **bear** *(accept)* --- to accept and deal with something unpleasant
- **close call** --- a bad situation you just managed to avoid
- **overdose** --- to take a dangerous amount of a drug at one time
- **911** --- the phone number in the US to call when there is an emergency
- **barista** --- a person who makes and serves drinks at a coffee shop
- **turn to somebody** --- to go to somebody for help
- **manual laborer** --- someone whose job involves physical work

English Short Stories for Intermediate Learners

- **largely** --- mostly
- **take root** *(idea)* --- to become accepted
- **meet with something** *(cause)* --- to cause a particular reaction
- **get into sth.** *(get involved)* --- to start being involved in sth.
- **C student** --- a student that is not good but not terrible
- **catch up** *(share)* --- to share and discuss personal news with sb.
- **sophomore** --- a second year student in high school or at college
- **language exchange** --- talking with sb. in two languages to practice
- **split up** *(separate)* --- to separate a group into smaller parts
- **converse** *[verb]* --- to have a conversation
- **pick up** *(learn)* --- to learn something with little to no effort
- **small talk** --- polite conversation about unimportant things
- **chatter** *(talk)* --- to talk about unimportant things
- **migrate** *(people)* --- to move to a new place to live and work
- **officially** *(formally)* --- in a way that everyone knows
- **speechless** --- so surprised or upset that you can't speak
- **fluently** *(speak)* --- speaking a foreign language very well
- **drop out** *(school)* --- to quit school without finishing
- **deciding** --- producing the final result of an event
- **occasionally** --- sometimes but not often
- **nothing short of** --- used to say something is important

- **out of something** *(because)* --- because of something
- **necessity** *(need)* --- the need for something
- **have nothing to prove** --- to feel you don't need to prove your value
- **desperately** *(very)* --- very (much)
- **burning** *(strong)* --- very strong
- **ego** *(sense of self)* --- your sense of your own importance

Comprehension Questions

1. What kind of family was Sarah born into?
    A) One filled with abuse and violence
    B) One filled with moderation and extremism
    C) One with mistreatment and leisure time
    D) One that was stable and protective

2. What kind of relationship did Sarah have with her brothers?
    A) She abused them to make herself feel better.
    B) She protected them from their mother.
    C) She ran away with them at age 16.
    D) She would get into intense shouting matches with them.

3. Sarah's friends at school did many things for her but did not...
    A) encourage her during class.
    B) make her laugh by cracking jokes.
    C) help her with her schoolwork.
    D) inspire her to go to college to become a doctor or lawyer.

4. Who would Sarah go to if she couldn't pay her bills?
    A) She would go to her parents who would support her.
    B) She would turn to her mother for help.
    C) She had nobody to go to.
    D) She had her friend Leah who would take care of her.

5. What kind of work does a barista do?
    A) They serve drinks for customers at a bar.
    B) They make drinks for customers at a coffee shop.
    C) They do heavy manual labor.
    D) All of the above

6. How did Sarah get started learning Spanish?
    A) She bought grammar books and memorized vocabulary.
    B) She had Gabriel help her at the language exchange.
    C) She had her customers at the coffee shop teach her Spanish.
    D) She used apps and listened to audio lessons.

7. What happened when Sarah spoke Spanish to her customers?
    A) She was insulted for not being a fluent speaker.
    B) She was full of surprise and joy.
    C) They were pleased and spoke back in Spanish.
    D) They replied that they speak English.

8. What do you typically do at a language exchange?
    A) You and a partner practice speaking in foreign languages.
    B) You practice languages in a classroom setting.
    C) You talk with someone about foreign languages.
    D) You trade your native language for a new one.

9. How did Gabriel get so good at so many languages?
    A) He traveled to multiple countries.
    B) He spent all his free time reading and listening to languages.
    C) He had a natural talent for languages.
    D) He read grammar books and listened to audio lessons.

10. Which of the following best describes language immersion?
    A) Learning a language because of extreme necessity
    B) A way to learn a language in moderation
    C) An extremely dedicated lifestyle to learn a language
    D) Learning a language because of moderate necessity

ABOUT THE AUTHOR

Language Guru is a brand created by a hardcore language enthusiast with a passion for creating simple but great products. They work with a large team of native speakers from across the world to make sure each product is the absolute best quality it can be.

Each product and new edition represents the opportunity to surpass themselves and previous works. The key to achieving this has always been to work from the perspective of the learner.

DID YOU ENJOY THE READ?

Thank you so much for taking the time to read our book! We hope you have enjoyed it and learned tons of vocabulary in the process.

If you would like to support our work, please consider writing a customer review on Amazon. It would mean the world to us!

We read each and every single review posted, and we use all the feedback we receive to write even better books.

ANSWER KEY

Chapter 1:
1) B
2) D
3) A
4) B
5) C
6) C
7) A
8) B
9) B
10) D

Chapter 2:
1) B
2) B
3) A
4) A
5) A
6) D
7) C
8) D
9) C
10) D

Chapter 3:
1) A
2) C
3) B
4) A
5) D
6) B
7) A
8) C
9) B
10) D

Chapter 4:
1) C
2) D
3) D
4) C
5) C
6) A
7) C
8) D
9) A
10) A

Chapter 5:
1) D
2) C
3) B
4) D
5) A
6) B
7) B
8) D
9) C
10) D

Chapter 6:
1) A
2) B
3) B
4) A
5) B
6) A
7) C
8) D
9) C
10) C

Chapter 7:
1) A
2) D
3) B
4) C
5) C
6) D
7) C
8) C
9) D
10) C

Chapter 8:
1) A
2) B
3) D
4) C
5) B
6) D
7) C
8) A
9) B
10) C

www.ingramcontent.com/pod-product-compliance
Lightning Source LLC
Chambersburg PA
CBHW030157100526
44592CB00009B/317